EL CERAMICO

THE STORY OF THE
POTTERIES DERBY

LIAM BULLOCK

First published by Pitch Publishing, 2023

Pitch Publishing
9 Donnington Park,
85 Birdham Road,
Chichester,
West Sussex,
PO20 7AJ
www.pitchpublishing.co.uk
info@pitchpublishing.co.uk

ISBN 978 1 80150 393 8

Typesetting and origination by Pitch Publishing

Printed and bound in Great Britain by TJ Books Limited, Padstow, Cornwall

Contents

About the Author

Liam Bullock is the author of the 2021 book *Twinned With Reykjavik: Stoke City FC: The Icelandic Years 1999-2006*. He has also published various scientific pieces and articles as part of his day job as a geologist. He continues to support Stoke City from afar in Spain with his wife Cris and dog Rex.

Contributors

BEFORE WE get stuck into tales and details of the Potteries derby, it's probably a good point to just confirm that I am indeed a Stoke City fan. A lifelong fan at that, born and raised in Applegarth Close at the top end of Fenpark, and schooled at Sandford Hill and St Thomas More in Longton. Does this mean that I'm going to write this book from a 100 per cent biased Potters perspective, giving a red-and-white-tinged slant to every debatable incident and with unabashed support of Stoke and detestation of Vale? Of course!

No, I kid. Have you met a Stoke supporter before? We love to give out about our own club in a negative way! Just spend two minutes reading the replies to the official team news at 2pm on Twitter on a Saturday. However, perhaps there are times where my own allegiances may unwittingly come into play and I view things from a Stoke City point of view. For that, I can only apologise in advance to Vale fans, and offer this as a way of mitigating against such biases.

I have sought the memories, recollections, thoughts, opinions and rants of supporters of both clubs for this book. Whether it's favourite memories, worst moments, personal recounts, history lessons or just a judgement on the Potteries derby as a whole, these wonderful contributors have helped to make this book into what I really want it to be: a view from the people of the city and the terraces, be them from Burslem or Blythe Bridge, the Railway Stand or the Boothen End. There will also be plenty of media quotes and recollections from players, managers and high-profile club associates scattered throughout.

As is often stated, it's the people who make Stoke-on-Trent, so the people also make the two professional football clubs of the city. Hopefully I can provide the play-by-play of the story from humble beginnings of the Potteries derby, through the fiercest years of the rivalry, right up to the situation as it is today (at time of writing at least), and the group of collective fans can provide the colour commentary. Here are our key contributors:

In the black and white corner

Ally Simcock: FSA board member, Port Vale fans' liaison officer and former chairwoman of the Port Vale Supporters' Club

Patrick Floyd: loyal and devoted Port Vale fan

Barry Seaton: Port Vale fan with 58 years of stories to tell

Tom, Kirsty and Dan: co-hosts of the *Ale and the Vale* podcast

In the red and white corner

Angela Smith: presenter on BBC Radio Stoke and member of Stoke City Fans Council

Peter Smith: chief Stoke City reporter for Stoke-on-Trent Live and *The Sentinel*

Ben Rowley: founder of *The YYY Files*, a Stoke City podcast

Foreword by Carl Dickinson

Stoke City 2002–2011, Port Vale
2013–2016, manager of Hanley Town
2021–2022

I FIRST joined Stoke when I was 14 or 15 after leaving Derby County. I managed to gain a scholarship in 2002 and ended up leaving in 2011. During this time, I was lucky enough to have played for the first team and be a part of a promotion-winning team in 2008 to the Premier League and then to be able to say – I'd played in the Premier League. I was still a young lad at this stage, being only 21, but I was part of an amazing group of people and changing room.

After leaving Stoke in 2011, little did I know that two years later I'd be back in Staffordshire, signing for Port Vale in 2013. There were a lot of discussions about whether this was the right thing to do or not, but with what had happened at my previous club, I felt that it was right to be back home! My first year at Vale was excellent, and we achieved a top-half finish. This led to me signing a new deal and being given the captain's armband, which I was truly thankful for.

I loved my time at both clubs. At Stoke, making my debut as a 17-year-old and then being part of that promotion group is something that I am so proud of, and very lucky to have achieved. With Vale, I enjoyed my time and probably played both the most football of my career and also my best football. I'm lucky enough to have an excellent relationship with both sets of fans, and I can't thank them all enough for the way they have been with me and my family over the years, particularly supporting me through the deaths of my parents.

I didn't know too much about the Potteries derby before joining Stoke. But once I had signed, I learned how intense it was, and how there had been some fierce battles over the years! Unfortunately I never got to experience being in a Potteries battle, but I know through speaking to fans, staff and players who had played in the fixture that the atmosphere was always incredible. I would have loved to have played in a game of this stature, as I think it is one of the higher-rated derbies in the country.

I would also love to see this fixture at some point in the future. I know the city would come alive to see one half in the famous red and white and the other half in the famous black and white go to battle.

Preface

Two Tribes

THERE ARE few more dramatic sights than the rising
cold mist against the blinding stadium floodlights on
the clear night sky in the middle of winter, especially
when heightened by the mixed rising smoke from
a fevered and full away stand. The Burslem streets
were littered with fluorescent police officers, roughly
one bobby for every 30 fans, prowling outside the riot
vans and numerous town centre pubs. One officer
described the mood as 'like waiting for two tribes to
go to war', to paraphrase a famous Frankie Goes to
Hollywood song. The local bars were open, but heavily
secured, with many sporting A4 sheets of paper in the
windows, printed with 'HOME FANS ONLY' in the
largest possible font sizes. The local park was locked
off to prevent any unfortunate meetings, and by early
evening, the queues began to form outside the red-
brick turnstiles.

Once inside, the pre-match atmosphere was already building and threatening to boil over before a ball had been kicked. Just about every rendition of the various anti-rival songs were exhausted before kick-off, with opposition fans seemingly crammed into their respective stands either side of the corner flag, not a single supporter sat down. Even more fluorescent-coloured security personnel marked the no man's land between the two stands, as stewards and yet more police donned the only colours more widespread than red and white or black and white – reflective bright yellow. 'We've been on the p*ss since 11 o'clock,' one fan boasted, 'got the day off work and me and the lads worked our way up through Sneyd Green and Cobridge, down to Burslem. Bouncer didn't ask who we supported, luckily for us!' Another fan simply stated, 'I can't stand these c***ts,' which was no doubt echoed on the other side of the divide. Among the waving arms of V signs, single middle digits and loose fists gesturing back and forth, a burst of applause broke through as the players took to the pitch.

In something of a modern-day rarity, both teams were led out by local captains; one an experienced, talismanic centre-forward, the other an aspiring midfield general at the start of his career. The handshakes (this time not a rude gesture directed at opposition fans, but actual handshakes), applause and formalities were dealt with, and it was time for kick-off. It didn't take long before the fireworks began on and off the pitch. Chances rained in from the home side after a couple of minutes, and the early pressure was rewarded as the local captain put his team ahead, before immediately lifting his shirt to the away end, to the backdrop of a chorus of rapturous cheers from the home stands. Of course, the pose was the typical response to the suggestive chant about the forward's perceived weight, though as in most cases, the suggestion may not have been entirely accurate, or was at the very least ironic coming from some of the stockier shouting supporters.

As the first half rumbled on, the home pressure continued, resulting in a second and third goal before the referee called a halt to the one-sided proceedings. From that point on, the match on the pitch became an afterthought, as the terraces came to be the centre of attention for the authorities and press representatives in the near-8,000 attendance.

The red-smoke pyrotechnics continued to blaze from the away stand, which created an almost Peter Jackson-directed feel to the ongoing battle of songs and hand signals. The Middle Earth backdrop became an even more fitting setting as projectiles of broken chairs, empty plastic Carling bottles, ignited smoke bombs and anything not nailed down (anymore) was launched over the rows of helmeted officers towards the home end and back again. If a catapult or battering ram could have been snuck in under a Stone Island jacket, I'm sure it would have been.

Pushing and scuffling with stewards and police began to break out, with fans climbing on chairs and over each other to get just that little bit closer to the action. Below the terraces, the away end was starting to literally crumble, as windows were smashed, toilet facilities uprooted, advertising boards ripped down and bins hurled across a floor now barely visible through all the scattered glass, plastic and beer. There were even attempts to start a fire in the away toilet block, which could have been a legitimate disaster had the instigator succeeded in doing so.

As the game ended, police clad in reinforced headwear and riot shields scrambled to keep the two sets of supporters separate in the streets, with major roads closed and drones deployed to monitor events from above. Even one of the highest-known police presences for any game in the country of that season couldn't prevent further trouble and damage, as cars were mounted, pub windows caved in, and fans looked to go head-to-head one last time.

In the aftermath, 11 arrests were made, 12 banning orders were dished out, and damage worth thousands of pounds was caused, with punishments dealt to culpable attendees of a shockingly wide age range of 18 to 61. The local authorities pointed towards the 'mindless violence, disorder and considerable damage', 'shocking levels of hostility' and 'despicable behaviour by a large number of fans'. It is even more telling to see the phrase 'large number of fans' used, as this level of football trouble is usually blamed on a 'minority of the crowd', which was somewhat predictably advocated by the representatives of the away team offenders. Visitors in the away end who witnessed the trouble, but did not get involved, took to social media as the dust, smoke and glass settled. 'Bonkers'. 'Embarrassing'. 'Unsavoury'. 'Dreadful night'. 'Bomb site'. 'Uneducated cavemen'. And that's just from your own fellow supporters.

* * *

So there went the most recent meeting of the two clubs at the time of writing. On the pitch, goals from Tom Pope, Luke Hannant and two from Cristian Montaño did the business for the home side. On Tuesday, 4 December 2018, it finished 4-0 to Port Vale against Stoke City's under-21s. Stoke City's under-21s. In the early stages of the EFL Trophy, under the Checkatrade sponsorship.

If that's a nothing game between a weakened Port Vale side and a Stoke City team of literal kids in a cup competition that the Potters shouldn't have even been a part of, that nobody cares about or even bothers to support up until the final stages, what would happen if the two clubs ever met in a *real* cup game? Or better yet, a *league* game?

1

A Tale of One City

TO FULLY understand the true nature of the Potteries derby, you first have to understand the city of Stoke-on-Trent itself. There are many, many aspects about Stoke-on-Trent and the surrounding areas that make it a most unique part of the UK. Most of us Stokies (or whatever some residents would prefer to be referred to as) probably go by for much of our early lives oblivious to these quirks and oddities, and it's only when we either venture beyond the borders of the ST postcode or immerse ourselves with people from outside our fair city that we become more aware of what makes Stoke-on-Trent 'different'.

I learned a lot about the traits of my own Potteries homeland when I first attended Keele University back in 2007. Being a Keele student presents a special position for a Stoke-on-Trent original, as you're able to stay local (Keele is a village on the outskirts of

Newcastle-under-Lyme, immediately neighbouring the city), but you're essentially surrounded by thousands of staff and students from all over the world. Generally, my interactions with Keele folk have been positive towards our city, with plenty of affection for the friendliness and character of the local people, and of course the widespread approval of oatcakes. There is also a lot of fun to be had with our accent, especially the use of the word 'duck' for affection, and the way that we pronounce book, cook and look (real emphasis on the 'oo' sound). But there are certain debates and quandaries that do consistently arise when discussing the area. For instance:

- **'Where even *is* Stoke-on-Trent?'**

OK, we can all find the city on Google Maps or junctions 15 and 16 off the M6, but more specifically, is Stoke-on-Trent in the Midlands? Is it in the north-west? Does Stoke-on-Trent count as 'the north'? We're part of the county of Staffordshire, so technically we are part of the West Midlands. But we're more or less on the upper limit of the Midlands, and historically, some locals would say we're more affiliated with the industrial and cultural heritage of the more northern towns and cities. We're a BBC *Midlands Today* and ITV *Central News* area, but you only have to travel a few miles up the road and you're into BBC *North West Tonight* and ITV *Granada Reports* territory. So maybe it depends on where you're situated in and around the city, or more typically, how you view yourself as a person.

It could come down to how the city residents vote. Historically it has always been a safe Labour seat, but even that has swung the other way in recent years. I would say that most locals I have spoken to don't really see themselves as Midlanders, even if we technically are. I'm also pretty sure that the rest of the Midlands doesn't really want us anyway. Then again, does the north-west? Perhaps we're just an enclave on the border, like Andorra between France and Spain.

Whether Stoke is in 'the north' depends on where you put the line between north and south. The newly formed Northern Independence Party has us down as some kind of demilitarised zone on the border, officially as a 'bordering area that we [the party] argue must be offered localised referendums on annexation'. So even the self-styled authority on the north doesn't know what we are.

Colloquially, some people put the border as anything north of Watford Gap, but in general, the imaginary line seems to start somewhere between Birmingham and Manchester. Once again, Stoke-on-Trent is in no man's land. These kinds of social, cultural and political anomalies have helped to make Stoke-on-Trent a very individualistic region. Are we Midlanders? Are we northerners or north-westerners? We're just Stokies. But the segregations don't start and stop at the city limits.

- **'Is Stoke-on-Trent a city?'**

Yes, and it has been since 1910. But not like a normal city, because we're made up of individual towns. Stoke-on-Trent is 'polycentric', with numerous centres, authorities and identities.

- **'OK, so how many towns? Five? Six?'**

There are six towns – Hanley, Burslem, Tunstall, Longton, Fenton and Stoke (aka Stoke-upon-Trent). There is some possible confusion as Arnold Bennett, the Hanley-born author of the late 19th and early 20th centuries, wrote novels that referred to 'The Five Towns', omitting Fenton from his stories (a bit of an insult to a Fentonian such as myself). Despite its immediate proximity to the city, Newcastle-under-Lyme is its own town with its own governance. Having lived there myself, a lot of 'castle residents do not wish to be referred to as part of Stoke-on-Trent.

- 'That's a little confusing. Presumably Stoke-upon-Trent is the city centre of Stoke-on-Trent?'

Well, no. The town of Stoke is the location of the main central government, and the main railway station, although even that's a little bit out of the town centre too. The principal commercial centre is Hanley. This is where you will find the main bus station and shopping centre.

* * *

That's just a sample of the kinds of peculiarities Stoke-on-Trent and Stokies face, and we haven't even got to the football teams yet! Stoke-on-Trent is the smallest city to house two Football League teams. Places with two clubs such as Birmingham, Bristol, Manchester, Sheffield and Nottingham all boast higher populations, while similarly sized areas such as Derby, Southampton, Coventry, Bradford and Hull are all one-team cities. The day-to-day mixing of the two sets of fans is not something that tends to happen to that degree in similar-sized cities. To put it simply: this city shouldn't really be big enough for the both of us. It's something that former Stoke City chairman Gunnar Gíslason openly stated in February 2003, and something that will be discussed later in this book.

Sharing a city with your main rival means it's inevitable that you'll also share schools, workplaces, pubs, gyms, supermarkets and basically any public place with them. You're very likely to share a classroom or a staff room with a Port Vale or Stoke City fan in the city, so escaping ridicule after a notable defeat is unlikely to happen. Conversely, a chance to strut around the office like a peacock on a Monday morning after a weekend victory is one to relish when the bloke in the corner cubicle has his club shop tat all over his desk. Non-uniform days and sports days at school meant many kids would don their replica shirts, posturing their way around the all-weather pitch. Perhaps the only thing more annoying than seeing a Vale or Stoke shirt on one of your mates was seeing a Manchester United or Liverpool shirt on them instead.

Living in a relatively small place that has a couple of league teams knocking about also means it can be quite claustrophobic when wrestling for local media attention. BBC Radio Stoke (and local commercial stations such as Signal Radio) will run matchday reporting that gives both teams, fans and managers fair time before and after their respective games, splitting the match coverage across multiple wavelengths. Local newspaper *The Sentinel* (known online as Stoke-on-Trent Live) will give back-page coverage to both teams, normally with the more significant report taking precedence over the story of lesser interest.

If all things are equal, Stoke City receive the bulk of the coverage due to having the larger fanbase. The difference in fanbase sizes can be a detriment to the local media in terms of what could be perceived as fair amounts of exposure. While the kind of balanced coverage that I have just outlined may seem like a fair compromise, there are still fans unhappy about sharing the airwaves with their neighbour, and accusations of unjust treatment from both parties. I've heard Port Vale fans complain about neglect from the local media, and I've heard Stoke City fans begrudge the amount of airtime Port Vale are afforded. I've overheard *The Sentinel* referred to as both 'The SentiVale' and 'The Stokenel' by both fanbases. 'How long do we have to listen to this bloke drone on?' on Radio Stoke's post-match phone-in *Praise and Grumble* could be relevant to either set of supporters, and also the manager interviews. We haven't even considered the reporting that Cheshire neighbours Crewe Alexandra are also granted in the local media outlets. Dario Gradi's breathless interviews seemed to run on forever. I guess the moral of the story for the local media for a city of two teams is that you can please some of the fans all of the time, you can please all of the fans some of the time, but you can't please all of the fans all of the time.

The other important geographical aspect that lends itself to the exceptional nature of the Potteries derby is the aforementioned six towns marvel. As well as sharing the city with the other team, there are also known territories for both teams. That means that the rivalry has both the 'shared city' aspect, but also the 'our area is better than your area' twist too, more typical of rivalries between teams of opposing towns and cities, such as Newcastle and Sunderland, and Southampton and Portsmouth. The city of Stoke-on-Trent isn't split 50/50 for Stoke and Vale fans. Generally, Burslem and Tunstall in the north of the city are the primary PVFC territories, while Longton, Fenton, Stoke and Hanley are more SCFC-dominated.

That's not to say all of Hanley is SCFC, or that Stoke and Vale fans don't live all over the city. Indeed, Port Vale were historically situated in Hanley, and parts of the city centre residential areas are very much Vale-dominated. But these general strongholds do exist. In both current and historic times, Burslem represents the home of Port Vale; the Mother Town is where Vale Park stands. Tunstall is the next town over to the north, meaning Vale is the closest team by proximity. Surrounding boroughs and villages can also boast a high number of Port Vale supporters, such as Biddulph, Bradwell and Bagnall. Stoke were historically based in the town of the same name, and now reside in the ST4 postcode on the outskirts of Stoke, Fenton and Longton. Surrounding towns such as Newcastle-under-Lyme, Leek, Stone, Kidsgrove and Blythe Bridge host a mixture of supporters, often weighted towards Stoke City.

One of my oldest friends, Patrick Floyd, grew up a Port Vale fan in Meir, very much a Stoke City bastion. When asked about his experiences as a kid in that area, Pat told me, 'I started following Vale in 2001. In Meir at 11 and 12, you had to be good at taking the banter as well as giving it, you just had to roll with it. It would have been easy to crumble, especially as everyone would say, "Don't be a Vale fan." It's simpler to not care when you're an adult, but when you're a kid, it would have been easy to say, "OK, I'll just support United, or Liverpool, or Stoke." I don't know how we managed to get any young supporters from that time in those areas. There was no infrastructure or foundations to entice the young kids. I became a Vale fan because I was taken to games by my uncle. I had even been to Stoke games before that, but something just didn't click with me. But when I went to Vale, it clicked.'

Ally Simcock, FSA board member, Port Vale fans' liaison officer and former chairwoman of the Port Vale Supporters' Club, echoed the notoriety of being a Valiant in Potters territory, 'It was difficult for me as a Vale fan because I tended to be the butt of the joke on many occasions and still am living in the south of the city. However, it spurred me on to really know my stuff. People underestimated me as a female football fan, and I made sure I could hold my own. I was taken to watch Vale first, so my team picked me. Now I'm loyal. As one of only two Vale fans in my year, it was great being able to have the upper hand, but if we lost, it was pure hell.

'The derby was an occasion, not just a match. You had a build-up for a couple of weeks where the other kids at school would be giving you grief. The excitement, the anticipation that anything could happen. This wasn't just about points, it was about pride! Walking to the game, I wasn't allowed to show my colours (living in Stoke, it wasn't recommended). Once in the ground though, my Vale top and scarf would be on show, and I would be singing loudly.'

Tom from the *Ale and the Vale* podcast grew up just on the outskirts of the city, and calls to mind the footprint that Stoke had over the area, 'Growing up in Clayton, at school, it was tough being a Vale fan. I think there was about five of us in a school of 1,000! I was ridiculed for most of it as we were in a lower division. One of the closest places to play football was also Stoke's training ground, so that didn't help!'

Kirsty, co-host of the pod, continues the shared Valiant feelings, 'Stoke fans used to give me stick all the time at school in the '90s. They'd walk around at primary school with their Stoke scarves in groups, holding them high and trying to get people to join them! But it was good because, as I got a bit older, Vale were genuinely better than Stoke. It was short-lived, but great years.'

Fellow *Ale and the Vale* co-host Dan grew up on the black and white side of the border, with a much more pleasant experience, 'I went to school in Burslem, and the majority of us were Vale fans, so it wasn't too bad at all. There was the odd Stoke fan, but I can't really remember any issues or trouble, as most of us followed Vale.'

The further out of the city you go, such as towards Stafford, Crewe, Macclesfield and Shrewsbury, the more diluted the Stoke-on-Trent representation becomes, mixing in with more proximal professional clubs and yet more support for more successful Premier League teams. It's quite poetic that the city of Stoke-on-Trent represents this grey area between the north and the south nationally, because parts of the city are similarly grey for Stoke and Vale areas. For me, the line pretty much straddles Leek New Road, separating Tunstall, Burslem and northern parts of Hanley from the rest of the city. There are pubs in parts of Sneyd Green, Abbey Hulton and Birches Head that have often run matchday coaches to both Stoke and Vale games, which suggests this is the area of the strongest mixture. Anywhere else, and you might just find yourself in enemy territory.

* * *

These lessons in local geography are meant to act as a bit of a scene-setter for the real factors that forged the Stoke City–Port Vale conflict – the actual football matches. The strong hatred hasn't always existed; it built over the years, with humble beginnings and a period of 'friendly' co-existence, through several players and managers crossing the divide, and eventual development into the fierce rivalry we know today – or at least, those of us who are affiliated with one of the two clubs know. A 2019 study named the Potteries derby as the 28th-biggest rivalry, below the likes of Doncaster Rovers v Rotherham United, Accrington Stanley v Morecambe, Cheltenham Town v Forest Green Rovers, and Crewe Alexandra v Port Vale. That simply won't do, and that's why I'm here writing this book, and righting this wrong. Yes, I'm a Stoke City fan, but this book isn't going to be all about Stoke's local triumphs. Let's face it, that would be a pretty short book. Besides, there is so much more that could, and should, be written.

It's time to delve into the history of the Potteries derby.

2

A Potted History

STOKE CITY and Port Vale are two of the oldest clubs in the English Football League. Stoke's history dates back to the 1860s, that much is for sure. Exactly when in the 1860s depends on who you ask. The club itself attributes its birth to 1863, with the formation of Stoke Ramblers. After a merger with Stoke Victoria Cricket Club, the name would later change to Stoke Football Club, and eventually Stoke City Football Club. However, some historians, and pretty much the entire Nottingham Forest fanbase, dispute the 1863 formation claim, suggesting the club actually formed in 1868, three years after Forest, which would make the Reds the oldest football club in the EFL (in the current Football League absence of Notts County).

Port Vale's own birth date is also disputed, although officially dated at 1876 by the club. Theories of the origin of their name span the more accepted versions, such as taking it from the valley of canal ports where the team played, or from taking their name from cricket clubs and Port Vale House, the venue of the inaugural meeting, to amalgamations of various merged club names, to the more speculative hypothesis that the club was basically named after a stack of local bricks! Again, concrete (not brick) evidence for their birth year is somewhat lacking, with documentation generally supporting an establishing year of 1878 or 1879. Either way, by around 1880, Stoke-on-Trent, or 'the Staffordshire Potteries area' (as the place was not yet an official federation of the six towns and was still some 40 years away from city status), had two football clubs, ready to start competing in friendlies, local league and cup competitions, and what would eventually become the Football League.

* * *

Though lacking in detail, the first reported meeting of the two teams occurred at Westport Meadows, nowadays known as Westport Lake and an early Burslem Port Vale home, prior to having to relocate due to subsidence and flooding. The first derby took place on 2 December 1882, in the second round of the Staffordshire Senior Cup. It was a competition that Stoke had already previously won two times since its inception in 1877, while Burslem Port Vale were a completely unknown quantity in the tournament. Despite their unfamiliar status, the Valiants, or perhaps more accurately 'nickname pending' (until 1919), secured a 1-1 draw against their more established opponents in what was helpfully described by the *Staffordshire Sentinel* (as it was then known) as 'a spirited game'. I doubt that there was any real rivalry between the two sides back then, but the draw must have felt sweet for the newcomers Vale. The euphoria would only last a week, though, as the replay saw the eventual Staffordshire Senior Cup runners-up Stoke FC run out 5-1 winners. The game was held at Stoke's new home, the Victoria Ground, located in the town of Stoke. 'The Vic' was originally constructed in an oval shape for athletics, with two grassy banks behind each goal and a compact wooden stand along Boothen Road.

The Vic hosted the first recognised major meeting between the two sides in 1887 in the first round of the FA Cup, in front of around 3,000 spectators. The first official Potteries derby goal came on the hour from George Lawton, a Stoke-born right-winger who would eventually represent both sides of the divide. The meeting was one of 17 between the two clubs from 1882 to 1890 that would finish in either a draw or a Stoke win. On 29 March 1890, Burslem Port Vale recorded their first win over Stoke at Cobridge's

Athletic Ground, triumphing 2-1 in front of an impressive attendance of 7,000.

Two years prior to Vale's first Potteries derby victory, Stoke FC, now a professional outfit and sporting the red-and-white-striped kit, became one of the 12 founding members of the Football League. Their early years were less than impressive, finishing bottom in the first two seasons, followed by a failure to be re-elected to the league in 1890. Their triumph in the Football Alliance led to re-election, where they remained until 1907, when relegation and bankruptcy saw Stoke spend several years in the district leagues of the Midlands and north-west. (Even back then they didn't know where Stoke-on-Trent should be situated.)

Vale did not fare much better at the time, initially becoming founder members of the Football League Second Division, but they were forced to resign from the league and liquidate in 1907. From the ashes of Burslem Port Vale rose the newly minted Port Vale, formed when minor league side Cobridge Church adopted the name and moved the club to the Old Recreation Ground in Hanley in 1912. The ground was located in the city centre on the site of what is now the Potteries Shopping Centre. Both teams rejoined the Football League in 1919, following the recommencement of football after the First World War.

Though league and FA Cup derby clashes were limited between the initial founding of the two clubs and eventual parting in the late 1950s, the two teams would regularly meet in any number of pre- and mid-season friendlies, testimonials, royal coronation events, club centenary celebrations, fundraisers, benefit matches, Christmas clashes and local cup competitions. Of course, at the end of the 19th century, these fixtures were highly important in establishing the teams both locally and regionally.

After benefitting from a head start of X number of years (let's say, at least eight), Stoke had verified themselves as the primary team in the Potteries. Victories in the Staffordshire Senior Cup had gone a long way to securing their status as the first choice of the six towns area.

Vale's initiation to the cup and plucky 1-1 draw in the first competitive local meeting had given the newcomers some much-needed exposure in the local press, helping establish them as the 'other' team of the area. Vale went on to win the North Staffordshire Charity Challenge in 1883 to cement their status, before going on to lose most of the friendly clashes between the two Potteries teams throughout the rest of the 19th century. In fact, it took 17 attempts for Vale to overcome their more sizeable neighbours, winning 2-1 at home on 29 March 1890.

The Potteries derby was growing in popularity, attracting 5,000 supporters for a friendly in 1893 advertised as 'the championship of the Potteries'. Staffordshire Senior Cup clashes kept the two teams familiar, as well as later meetings in the North Staffordshire and District League, the Birmingham Cup, the North Staffordshire Nursing Society Cup, the Hanley Cup, the May Bank Cup, North Staffs Infirmary Cup, Football League North Cup, Supporters' Club Trophy and the Wedgwood Trophy. Prizes for these tournaments included everything from trophies and plaques, to flowerpots, Greek figures and smokers' sets.

Derby friendlies and local or regional cup clashes basically became an annual thing right up to the early 1990s, and while they didn't generally attract that much interest, they still provided opportunities for feelgood moments and local bragging rights. Stoke took the two Christmas encounters in 1917 and 1918, and racked up an 8-1 win on 12 October 1918, a record for the Potteries derby and a scoreline more reminiscent of pre-season friendly clashes of these days with the likes of Newcastle Town. The best detail of the friendly and regional cup fixtures can be found in Jeff Kent's excellent compilation of Potteries derby encounters, *The Potteries Derbies*. To repeat the match reports here wouldn't do his fine hard work justice.

His 19th-century recounts include a clash which was abandoned after 30 minutes due to a hurricane, matches played in blizzards, broken ribs for a goalkeeper in a friendly, pre-goal-line technology goalmouth scuffles, pitch invasions (by fans and dogs), 'the most woeful exhibition of refereeing ever seen' and even a Rory Delap-esque goal straight from a throw-in.

* * *

In 1911, Stoke and Vale took their rivalry from the real world into the fictional world of Arnold Bennett. The Stoke-on-Trent novelist penned his classic work *The Card* with his typical world building akin to the Potteries area, which included two football teams – Knype (based on Stoke) and Bursley (Vale). Here is an extract:

'There were two "great" football clubs in the Five Towns – Knype, one of the oldest clubs in England, and Bursley. Both were in the League, though Knype was in the first division while Bursley was only in the second. Both were, in fact, limited companies, engaged as much in the pursuit of dividends as in the practice of the one ancient and glorious sport which appeals to the reason and the heart of England. (Neither ever paid a dividend.) ... Now, whereas the Knype Club was struggling along fairly well, the Bursley Club had come to the end of its resources. The great football public had practically deserted it. The explanation, of course, was that Bursley had been losing too many matches. The great football public had no use for anything but victories. It would treat its players like gods – so long as they won. But when they happened to lose, the great football public simply sulked. It did not kick a man that was down; it merely ignored him, well knowing that the man could not get up without help ... If it could see victories it would pay sixpence, but it would not pay sixpence to assist at defeats.'

Fortunately for Stoke fans, Bursley's 1-0 win over Knype didn't make it into the official record books.

* * *

Stoke and Port Vale had met in friendlies and various regional competitions on at least 89 reported occasions by the start of 1920. The (presumably) much anticipated first league encounter between the two teams occurred on 6 March 1920, a rainy Second Division clash at the Old Recreation Ground. Vale had found their feet in the league, but Stoke were the more established team, and the game ended in a 3-0 win for the visiting Potters. I assume the game was hotly anticipated, as 22,697 filled the stadium to capacity, with thousands more turned away from an hour before kick-off. In scenes evocative of Stoke City's return to the Premier League in the late 2000s, clusters of fans gathered at various viewing points outside of the ground to watch the game.

The return fixture took place a week later at the newly refurbished Victoria Ground, finishing 0-0 in front of a record crowd of around 27,000.

League football through the 1920s saw both teams enjoying prolonged spells of consecutive wins; four for Stoke between 1921 and 1923, and five for Vale between 1924 and 1927. Of the 23 league and FA Cup meetings between 1920 and 1933, only four ended in a draw, with 11 wins for Stoke and eight for Vale. Attendances during that time were generally around the 20,000 mark, dropping off a little bit to 14,000 for an FA Cup first round clash in 1922, and peaking at a league meeting in 1928, with 35,288 packed into the Victoria Ground.

The league meeting in March 1933, which ended Vale 1 Stoke City (now) 3, was a significant occasion, as it was the first City league goal for one Stanley Matthews. The exciting winger had previously made his mark on the Potteries derby a year prior in a North Staffordshire Royal Infirmary Cup tie, but the league meeting was a true highlight. The March fixture was also the last league match between the two sides at the Old Recreation Ground, and the last in the league between the two teams for 18 years as Stoke moved up to the First Division, leaving Vale behind in the second and third tiers until the two teams renewed acquaintances in the 1950s. Matthews would continue to shine in assorted friendlies, wartime leagues and regional tournaments between the two clubs in the late 1930s and the early to mid-1940s, playing alongside the likes of fellow England internationals Frankie Soo, Neil Franklin and Freddie Steele.

* * *

Though those early clashes between the two teams are not considered the height of the rivalry, there were still several noteworthy incidents that caught the attention of news outlets and even local authorities. As early as 1887 there were reports of Stoke fans 'howling and yelling like a pack of wolves' towards Vale players making their way back to their hotel. Fan, player and even refereeing scuffles also became more prevalent throughout the 1900s and 1910s. In 1886/87, Hanley-born goalkeeper Billy Rowley made the switch from Burslem Port Vale to Stoke. This wasn't an uncommon move back in the day. Most players were local lads anyway, and Rowley had already made the switch in the other direction three years earlier. However, the move came several months after Rowley, at that time still representing Vale, had two of his ribs broken by the Stoke front line in a friendly that ended 3-1 to Stoke. The story goes that Rowley required a small amount of whisky to be revived after the incident. In the aftermath, Vale were unhappy with how the 'friendly' had transpired, particularly for their established goalkeeper, and took the matter to the courtroom. As a result, Stoke were forced to pay £20, the equivalent of around £2,700 in today's money, to charity.

Another goalkeeping incident occurred on 23 April 1910, when Sunderland's Dickie Roose, who had previously turned out for Stoke in two spells between 1901 and 1907, appeared as a star guest player for Vale in a Potteries derby North Staffordshire and District League decider. His appearance was an act of revenge against the Stoke board with whom Roose had dramatically fallen out, in particular Stoke's chairman, Rev. A.E. Hurst. As well as showing up as a ringer against the Stoke reserves, Roose was also sporting his old Stoke shirt, which he refused to remove despite the referee's orders, riling up the 7,000 Stoke fans in attendance. Roose went on to put in a man-of-the-match display, in which his performance was described as saving 'every shot with such arrogant ease that the furious crowd spilled on to the field, only the brave intervention of the local constabulary saving him from a ducking in the River Trent'. Among the encroachers was the aforementioned Hurst, who ended up getting knocked out by one of his own forwards. Unsurprisingly, the match was abandoned at 2-0 to

Vale, who also fielded forward Herbert Chapman as another surprise starter. Fans had surrounded Roose and carried him towards the River Trent, with Stoke player Vic Horrocks knocked unconscious while trying to intervene. Roose was eventually rescued, but the match couldn't be saved.

Roose was no stranger to controversy at the time, famed for billing Stoke £31 for a private train to Aston Villa after missing his initial departure time. He later claimed that he thought the important league clash was actually a friendly, although even a friendly can still land you with two broken ribs. *The Sentinel*'s chief Stoke City writer Pete Smith has subsequently reflected on 'Roose-gate', 'If I could have been at any derby game, I'd probably choose that Staffs League decider in 1910 when Dickie Roose came back as a ringer. The audacity of it and the disbelief and fury from the Stoke fans must have been extraordinary.'

In the 1920s there were even discussions about a merger of the two clubs, with young estate owner and millionaire director John Slater making the attempted unification as part of his planned purchase of the county cricket ground in the town of Stoke. Vale fans were pivotal in thwarting Slater's attempts, the first of two merger considerations that would rally the supporters into responsive action (more on others later).

* * *

The 18-year absence of a league Potteries derby was ended on 6 January 1951 in the FA Cup first round in front of a whopping 49,500 spectators at the Victoria Ground. The huge attendance was treated to a 2-2 draw on 'a pudding of a pitch', resulting in a replay two days later, also played at the Vic, which saw Stoke run out 1-0 winners. The replay was held on a Monday afternoon, but still managed to attract 40,977 fans as thousands were given time off work to attend providing they completed their work tasks beforehand or afterwards. Despite the fixture being a replay, the game was not switched to Port Vale, which meant Stoke City would have to wait a little while longer before making their Vale Park debut.

In 1950, Port Vale had moved into their new home in Burslem, where they remain to this day. The ground was built on a former clay pit and coal mining area, typical of much of Stoke-on-Trent thanks to the underlying Carboniferous geology. The Vale Park plans were highly ambitious, and the development was dubbed the 'Wembley of the North', with talks of a capacity of up to 80,000, the laying of the most expensive pitch in the country and space for 1,000 parked cars. The nickname became a bit of a running joke, particularly in the red and white half of the city, but the capacity did reach half of the ambitious target, although the initial drive for 'lifetime seat' supporters, offering 200 games for £100, attracted fewer than 100 takers. Notwithstanding the bold claims about the sophistication of the new ground, the newly built Vale Park's drainage system was not quite capable of handling the January rainfalls and melting snow, meaning both the original tie and subsequent replay were switched to Stoke's home. This was a rare ground-switching occurrence that would repeat itself in a Potteries derby many years later.

The impressive attendances were an indication of how far Potteries football had come by the early 1950s. Stoke were coming off the back of a relatively successful spell following the end of the Second World War, coming agonisingly close to winning the First Division in 1947, but missing out after a final-day defeat to Sheffield United. Following that, and coinciding with the departure of Stanley Matthews, Stoke's performances and league positions declined, leading to relegation in 1953.

During the same period, Vale were experiencing the height of their successes, winning the Third Division North title and reaching the semi-finals of the FA Cup in 1954, only denied a place in the final by a controversially disallowed Albert Leake goal for offside. From 1951 to 1957, the Valiants were managed by Hanley-born Freddie Steele, a celebrated former striker of both Stoke and Vale who scored a whopping

140 goals in 224 appearances for the Potters over a long career at the Victoria Ground from 1933 to 1949, where he became the stadium's highest ever scorer. Steele joined Vale as player-manager, turning their fortunes and delivering their biggest successes to date (then and now), setting records and winning over the locals. The average home attendances soared to over 20,000 by 1954, the highest average in Vale's history. Steele would remain at the club until relegation in 1957, but would return for a second managerial spell in the early 1960s.

The early 1950s decline of Stoke City and parallel rise of Port Vale meant that the two clubs renewed league acquaintances on 4 September 1954, after more than two decades apart in divisional status. The much-anticipated reunion at the Victoria Ground was another mega-attendance, an all-ticket event in front of 46,777, many of whom arrived on specialist trains and buses, or purchased tickets from touts. Naturally, the game ended 0-0, the highlight of which was probably the pre-match performance of the Stoke-on-Trent Special Constabulary Band.

The first Potteries derby at Vale Park took place on 25 April 1955. Frank Bowyer scored the only goal in the second half to seal a 1-0 win for Stoke in yet another drab affair. To this day, the crowd of 41,674 is still Port Vale's record league gate. Indeed, the 40,000-

plus attendances for the derbies at both the Victoria Ground and Vale Park between 1951 and 1955 would never be achieved again, as numbers remained high for the middle part of the 1950s.

Lifelong Port Vale fan Barry Seaton discussed the ups and downs for the Valiants in the 1940s and '50s, leading up to the 1955 derby at Vale Park: 'Port Vale have had some grim years, but 1943 was the worst. There was a war on, the club had almost lost its name, the financial situation was dire, and William Huntbach died. He was president and the main reason for any income. When his estate called in his debentures, the club was destitute. The only course was to sell the Hanley Rec to the council. No name (almost), little income, no ground. New chairman William Holdcroft then took a course which would have daunted even the Glazers. After the war, he negotiated a price for 170 acres of wasteland just off Burslem town centre. The plan – a 70,000-seater stadium, the "Wembley of the North". Amazingly, he found backers. The club rented the Rec and began work on the grandiose project – with its own railway station, tenders for England internationals, access to Hamil Road from the station and bigger gates as the Potteries spread its wings.

'Gradually, the ground rose from the wasteland – a sprawling concrete, almost sci-fi creation, with hardly any cover whatsoever. The postwar attendances and player sales were profitable, and Vale kicked off at Vale Park in 1950 before 30,000 and a 1-0 win over Newport. We were still alive. Even rising again. Eventually permission was granted to use the Rec stand as cover and in 1955 the first Potteries derby at our home took place. It was a messy, scruffy affair in the wind and rain with a winner by Frank Bowyer on the hour for City. Home fans were pleased with Steele's promoted side and the effort given and this has become the minimum requirement for Valeites. The attendance was 41,674. Another fortune in the coffers of our plucky club. In the close season, Mr Holdcroft died aged 72. He had saved the club.'

By late 1955, the league and FA Cup meetings between the two teams since their reunion at the start of the decade were weighing in Stoke's favour, with two wins and two draws. Stoke had also won the last two league encounters of the early 1930s, meaning it was six games, and 23 years, since Vale recorded a competitive victory over Stoke.

The 1955/56 season was shaping up well for the two teams, with both Stoke in third place and Vale in fifth, eyeing up promotion to the First Division. The 8 October 1955 clash at Vale Park saw Vale's Scouse centre-forward and prolific goalscorer, Cyril Done, prod home after just five minutes, followed by a typically resolute defensive performance by Freddie

Steele's famed 'Iron Curtain' defence, aka the 'Steele Curtain'. As well as the 37,261 in attendance, thousands were also listening in across the North Staffordshire Royal Infirmary, the City General, Haywood Hospital and Stanfield Sanatorium on the new Broadcasts to Hospitals Service. The victory would be Vale's only one during the 1950s, as the remaining three league games finished 1-1, 3-1 to Stoke at the Vic and finally 2-2 at Vale Park in 1957.

That 3-1 result on the Wednesday night of 10 October 1956 was the first league game played at the Victoria Ground under the newly installed £15,000 floodlights. Eventually half of these floodlights would eventually cross the city divide, purchased by Vale in 1997.

By the 29 April 1957 fixture, during which Freddie Steele netted for the home team, the Vale Park attendance had dropped to around 22,000, as Vale slid back down to the Third Division and not long after, into the newly founded Fourth Division. Stoke would eventually see improved league and cup performances in the 1960s with the appointment of Tony Waddington and hugely significant return of 46-year-old Stanley Matthews. The friendlies and local cup ties would continue, but the two clubs would not meet in the league again for 32 years.

3

Absence Makes the
Heart Grow Fonder

THE YEARS that followed for Stoke City were highly successful, known as 'the Waddington years' between 1960 and 1977. However, the period of time was a highly tumultuous one for Port Vale. Though the two teams were kept well apart in both league and cup meetings (and eventually with friendlies becoming more sporadic), there were some curious crossovers between them. In July 1965 the recently retired and newly knighted Sir Stanley Matthews became Port Vale's new general manager, working alongside player-manager Jackie Mudie. His appointment came at a time when the Valiants were struggling on and off the pitch. The club were back in the Fourth Division and facing financial difficulties after a loss of more than £15,000 during the previous year. The appointment of Sir Stan was a huge boost to Vale supporters, as 'the

Wizard of the Dribble' was one of the most recognised and prestigious figures in British football, famed for his footballing brain, silky skills, his revolutionary approach to conditioning and his overall unmatched level of professionalism. He was a follower of Port Vale in his early years but had also become Stoke City's favourite son.

Quite peculiarly, Matthews wasn't issued a formal contract and had agreed to work unpaid, claiming only expenses, his way 'to give something back to the game that had given so very much to me'. Part of that giving back was reflected in his plans for a managerial ethos that he set out at Vale, to produce and nurture young local talent that would rise through the ranks and eventually move on for a large profit. It was, and still is, an approach that can be highly successful, if the long-term plan is just that – long-term. An unfortunate but not uncommon issue with the approach is short-term failure, and this plagued Matthews' stint at Vale Park, particularly at the very beginning. He started with two defeats (in front of large crowds) and ended the season in 19th position (in front of meagre crowds). In 1967, Mudie left citing personal reasons, though the underlying cause was thought to be that the Vale board were unwilling to show the patience for the youth policy to take effect. The dire financial situation was weighing heavily on the club, and there was a need for instant success and returns. Matthews stayed on as first team manager, sticking to his plans and principles, but Vale's financial perils caught up with them by November 1968. They were found to be in breach of six financial regulations, including illegal payments, wages and bonuses, resulting in a £4,000 fine and eventual exclusion from the Football League. Matthews was tasked with leading the club to the end of the season, with everyone involved already aware of their upcoming punishments.

Following their dismal campaign and eventual exclusion, Port Vale applied for re-election back to the Football League. The efforts required a lot of schmoozing and buddying up to the existing league clubs, who would ultimately decide the Valiants' fate. Surprisingly, it was Stoke City chairman Albert Henshall who stepped up to back the Burslem club. Meanwhile, Matthews was, for the first time in his life, using his name value and standing in the sport to garner support. The efforts were ultimately successful as Vale were reinstated into the Fourth Division, but not without cost. The support they had garnered came at the price of a total upheaval of the club's administrative hierarchy, including the changing of the chairman, board of directors, secretary and, yes, the manager. Matthews resigned in May 1968, taking up a scouting and youth team role instead. He was still owed £10,000 in unpaid salary and expenses, only receiving around £3,000 of the total amount, while the remaining £7,000 was written off.

The whole saga was a bit of a black mark on Sir Stan's illustrious career in the British game. All-time leading Port Vale appearance maker Roy Sproson once commented, '[Matthews] trusted people who should never have been trusted and people took advantage of him. I am convinced a lot of people sponged off him and, all the while, the club were sliding.' Matthews himself later said, 'The whole incident left a sour taste in my mouth, and I turned my back on management in English football forever … my time with Port Vale had ended with a chastening experience.'

It's interesting to note that Matthews felt that 'big clubs' such as Manchester United had received preferential treatment over the likes of Port Vale in terms of financial regulations and punishments. It's an argument that, in 2021, teams like Derby, Wigan, Bury, Bolton and Macclesfield could sympathise with, especially when their respective punishments were compared to that of the so-called 'Super League' teams.

The good news from the fallout of Sir Stan's managerial spell was that he would continue to build his already well-established legacy throughout the 1970s, supporting projects and coaching youth football across poverty-stricken areas of Africa. But the sour experience at Vale Park may have resulted in a big loss for British football, losing a young (in terms of a managerial career), innovative and success-driven man like Sir Stanley Matthews. It would have been great to see him take charge of Stoke City somewhere down the line, but it wasn't to be.

* * *

Vale floated in the third and fourth tiers for much of the 1960s and '70s, bottoming out at 20th in the Fourth Division in 1979/80, 88th overall and their record low finish. Prior to that, on 17 January 1976, there was an unusual occurrence at Vale Park. Middlesbrough were the visitors to Burslem and a crowd of 21,009 were on hand to witness a 1-0 win for the home side. But the home side wasn't Port Vale, it was Stoke City. In a move reciprocal to the help that the Stoke higher-ups had offered to the Valiants the previous decade, the Port Vale board had permitted the Potters to play the game at Vale Park after the Victoria Ground's Butler Street Stand roof had suffered severe damage from hurricane-force winds. The gale had also caused £2,000 of damage to Vale Park, but the destruction caused to the Butler Street Stand would severely affect the Potters then and arguably to this very day.

After the storm, the Vic was declared unsafe to host the upcoming cup tie with Tottenham Hotspur and subsequent league clash with Boro. The FA Cup match with Spurs was postponed until a later date, but the league game was still an unresolved issue. In a charitable show of class, Port Vale chairman Mark Singer offered the use of Vale Park to his Stoke City counterpart Albert Henshall, who was grateful to accept the offer, and successfully sought official permission from the Football League to switch the Middlesbrough game to Burslem. This was, and at time of writing still is, the only top-flight football match played at Vale Park. *The Sentinel*'s correspondent Peter Hewitt wrote, 'The game will be remembered for the occasion rather than the quality. Moores [the goalscorer] was finally rewarded for his perseverance with a goal ... to reward the fans who had made their way into "foreign territory".' Stoke favourite Alan Hudson commented, 'Vale have a great setup. The players have their own room with a colour television, but what they need is more atmosphere from bigger gates.'

The attendance was more than three times higher than the highest home attendance for any Port Vale game for that season, and was even higher than the next three Stoke fixtures at the repaired Victoria Ground. Port Vale secretary Richard Dennison stated, 'We had to show we could cope when our normal 4,000 gate became 20,000. We had our problems through storm damage – toilets and turnstiles damage, pieces of asbestos all over the place. Football is all about making friends and helping people. It was right we should go out of our way to help.' The good feeling between Stoke and Vale continued to April of 1976, where the teams met in a friendly to celebrate Port Vale's centenary, a game that finished 1-1, lit up by the performance of Stoke's Jimmy Greenhoff.

For Stoke, the legacy of the storm and stand damage wasn't restricted to the one game at Vale Park. The repair bill of nearly £250,000 had put the Potters in deep financial trouble, which could only be resolved by the sale of several key players, including Greenhoff, Alan Hudson and Mike Pejic. After a stellar start to the 1970s, which saw Stoke win the League Cup (the only major trophy in their history), reach the FA Cup semi-final on two occasions and compete in the UEFA Cup, Stoke were relegated in the 1976/77 season. Tony Waddington left after a 1-0 defeat to Leicester at the Vic in March 1977. Alan Durban led Stoke back to the First Division in 1978/79, but their top-flight stay was ended in dramatic fashion in 1984/85. The season would become known by Stoke fans under the unfortunate moniker of 'the Holocaust season'. Of their 42 league games, Stoke won three, drew eight and lost 31. They finished bottom on 17 points, a mere 23 points behind 21st-placed Sunderland and 33 points behind 19th-placed Queens Park Rangers. Notably, two of the three victories actually came against Manchester United and Arsenal. After dropping out of the First Division, the Potters wouldn't return to dine at the top table again until 2008.

Over in the north of the city, Port Vale promoted assistant manager John Rudge to the top job in December 1983, with the club once again heading towards the bottom tier of the Football League. After the initial and inevitable relegation, Rudge steadied the ship and led Vale to two promotions in three years, with a famous cup win against Tottenham Hotspur along the way. After a 32-year absence, 'Rudgie' led Port Vale back to the Second Division in 1989. It was time for another reunion with Stoke City, and the friendships and goodwill built up over that time were about to come to an end.

4

A Rivalry Renewed

FROM THE early 1960s up to the late 1980s, Stoke and Vale found themselves kept apart in league meetings, meaning the relationship had become more of a 'friendly' rivalry than any true hatred or disdain for each other. In fact, it was pretty unexceptional for Stoke-on-Trent footballing fans on either side of the divide to attend the home games of the other team while their first love was out on the road. The healthy relationship gave fresh life to the pre-season friendlies and local cup competitions, which were annual occurrences during the time apart in league status.

The Potteries football 'scene' of that time was lyrically described by Vale fan Barry Seaton, 'My brother, Chris, exemplifies the Vale–Stoke relationship in the late 1960s. Aged 14, he became a red and nagged Tony Waddington for a Junior Supporters' Page [in the match programme]. When the great man relented, suddenly there was a photo of Paisley-shirted Chris, all his mates' letters in *The Ceramic City Clipper*, and even a John Mahoney Fan Club. By 1972 there were two tickets for the League Cup Final, which he had to miss. They passed to me in London, and I was close to Eastham as the Stoke City winner went in. I was overjoyed. Chris was also overjoyed for Vale home wins when he was with us in the club bar, eating Burgess burgers and playing dominoes and darts. This sort of thing was not exceptional.

'The 1960s was generally derby-free. The return of [Stanley] Matthews elevated Stoke to new heights of fame and achievement, while Vale got stuck in the Third Division and even went down to the basement just as Stoke were back in the top division. By 1968 the "Slaughter of the Innocents" almost ended Port Vale full stop, when tea-sets were given to parents of promising boys, contrary to regulations. All agreed that expulsion from the league was severe. The Old Pals' Act ensured re-election.

'Relations between the clubs were cordial and fans had nothing to hate. With [Jimmy] McIlroy, [Dennis] Viollet, Matthews and [Tony] Allen, Stoke had star status. Vale relied on cast-offs and vets. It was quite regular for fans like me to go to Vale one week and Stoke the next – without rancour. Stoke was Jimmy Dean; Vale was Jimmy Clitheroe. We tended to be patted on the school cap. The derby was not mooted until 1970 when Vale won a brilliant game 3-2 to celebrate the City Festival. Six years later, the centenary of Vale attracted almost 10,000 to Burslem just as the gap between the teams was narrowing. The good feeling ushered in a series of close-season friendlies. There was the Wedgwood Trophy, games for Phil Sproson and Russell Bromage and the unfortunate Chris Maskery. Lee Chapman and the largely forgotten Jeff Cook netted hat-tricks. By 1987, the clubs were almost eating from the same table and the time was ready for the resumption of the Potteries derby. It was 23 September 1989.'

* * *

Yes, as the 1980s came to an end, both Potteries teams were back in the Second Division. Stoke City were now under the stewardship of Mick Mills, who would be replaced by Alan Ball later in 1989, the fifth manager in ten years. The Potters were stagnating, with the infamous 1984/85 season still fresh in the memory of supporters and any remaining players and staff. Over in Burslem, Port Vale were a team on the up, with a promising side and enjoying life under John Rudge; even Stoke legend Mike Pejic was part of the setup at Vale Park. The Valiants had amassed a squad of names that would become familiar to both sets of fans for many years to come, including mainstay goalkeeper Mark Grew, committed defenders Neil Aspin and Dean Glover, attacking midfielder and former Stoke City youth prospect Robbie Earle, the energetic Andy Porter and goalscorers Darren Beckford and Nicky Cross. Stoke's squad included the likes of the ever-present goalkeeper Peter Fox, popular defenders Ian Cranson, Lee Sandford and John Butler, the soon-to-be national treasure Chris Kamara, local lad Carl Beeston and up front, their main source of goals, Wayne Biggins.

Despite the different feelings in the two camps, City were still the well-established 'big team' of Stoke-on-Trent when the first competitive meeting in 32 years rolled around at the Victoria Ground on 23 September 1989. Even the majority of summer friendlies had gone in Stoke's favour over the preceding years. The local press had referred to Stoke as the 'big brother' in the lead-up to the clash. As Earle put it in his September 2019 *Sentinel* column when recounting, 'Before that game it was a case of, "Here's little Vale, coming for their big day out." We were better than that and we were looking forward to the chance to prove it.' There was no doubt that the city was fired up. The highest gate of the season of 27,004 eclipsed league game attendances against the likes of West Ham, Leeds, West Brom and Newcastle, including a sold out away following behind the goal in the Stoke End, spreading across to the perpendicular paddock. It was actually the biggest home gate for seven years, since Liverpool visited the Vic in the top flight, so there was no doubt that this meant everything to the fans. Stoke-on-Trent had ground to a halt for the return of the Potteries derby.

The two teams lined up like this:

Stoke City: Fox, Butler, Statham, Kamara, Cranson, Beeston, Ware, Palin, Bamber, Morgan, Beagrie.

Port Vale: Grew, Webb, Hughes, Mills, Aspin, Glover, Porter, Earle, Futcher, Beckford, Jeffers.

The first 45 minutes was a tense affair, with Vale just edging it in control and tempo, no doubt the happier of the two teams at the break. The game sprang into life in the second half, and just five minutes after the resumption Earle opened the scoring for the Valiants. The game and the goal must have meant just that little bit extra to Earle, who had grown up in the city, had attended Longton High School and watched plenty of games at the Vic. He was on Stoke's books from the age of 12 to 16, and after recovering from a broken leg he was presented with a deal to go part-time professional before John Rudge offered him a better chance of breaking through the ranks at Vale Park. Though he has claimed otherwise, there must have been an element of wanting to prove Stoke wrong for not showing the faith in him that the Vale eventually would. Earle latched on to a through ball from John Jeffers to put Vale ahead in front of the ecstatic away fans.

The lead would only last for 15 minutes, however, as the much-maligned Dave Bamber got on the end of a Gary Hackett cross to knock the ball into the path of Leigh Palin, whose shot wickedly deflected off Alan Webb to give the Stoke midfielder the first of his three goals within a month, his total tally for the season. The visitors felt that they should have gone ahead again, after Jeffers chased down an Earle through ball on the left wing, beating goalkeeper Fox to the ball and crossing for Ron Futcher to power a header towards goal. The ball struck the bar, and Ronnie Jepson headed the rebound wide with the goal gaping. The woodwork would be rattled again but this time in front of the Boothen End, as Ian Cranson's header beat the goalkeeper but not the post. Stoke finished strongly, but the game ended 1-1.

Both teams left with mixed feelings. Either could have come away with zero or three points, but Vale were the happier of the two sides. Earle recounted, 'As I remember it, that 1-1 draw lived up to the hype. We could have won it when Ronnie Jepson had a header that would have made him Lord Ronald of Burslem had it gone in ... We came off a little disappointed not to have won it, but I think people respected us more after that, took us more seriously.

We weren't seen as little old Vale anymore; we were a good side.'

After the game, Rudge said, 'For an hour, we played some tremendous, controlled football and just lacked the breakthrough in the first half. We could have easily won the game, but in the second half they put us under some pressure … Stoke's goal was a deflection off Alan Webb which I thought was a bit cruel on us. But I'm sure the supporters will be proud of our performance. It proves that we have closed the gap on Stoke and are now competing on equal terms.'

Stoke manager Mick Mills said, 'Vale did not surprise me. They were the best footballing side to come out of Division Three last term and when you play them you know they are going to knock the ball around. This was their big game of the season, and we knew it would be tight, as local derbies so often are. Both teams played good football, but I felt we gave them too much freedom in the first half.'

The day's events were largely overshadowed by an eruption of crowd trouble around the city throughout the day. The epicentre of the violence was at a Burslem pub, The Huntsman, where fans clashed after the game in 'an orgy of violence', resulting in the arrests of 85 individuals. Former Vale central defender Neil Aspin would later comment, 'I didn't realise how great the rivalry was until we played each other for the first time. It is a massive game if the two teams ever play.'

Vale fan Barry Seaton recounted his memories of the day, 'Marston's Pedigree, top-class cheese and onion cobs at Uncle Tom's Cabin and me and Todd were ready to join 27,000 at the Victoria Ground for the most-hyped game in the series. It was the Second Division; both teams had started OK, but Vale had star man Ray Walker, recovering from injury, on the bench. Conditions were perfect, pitch superb and Simon Mills took the game over in Walker's place. Straight-backed, balding, he played at his own stately pace and passed like a dream – in went Jeffers, Hughes, Beckford and for an hour it was beyond our every expectation except that it was 0-0. Then – yards from us – Jeffers found Earle in the Stoke End area. A pirouette, a sashay to the right, an Agüero step and a perfect shot past Fox. Cue disbelief, a break in the space-time continuum, loss of limb control and ecstasy. Only this moment mattered. I could die happy. After 26 years of Halifax, Darlington and Barrow, here was justification for everything.

'Of course, it didn't last; it was only 1-0. Now a Stoke midfielder, exasperated, reddened of face, and humiliated by Mills, started to win tackles, and charge up the middle of the field. It was Chris Kamara. Unbelievable, knees pounding, dragging City upfield. Debutant Palin shot, had a lucky deflection – 1-1.

Walker entered the fray and had time to set up Jepson for a header which was wide. Poor old Ronnie never did score for Vale. We didn't know whether we were happy, sad or both. But the memories of that Mr Mills hour and Earle goal will never fade. It had been my first live derby and I fervently hoped the clubs would stay in the same division.'

* * *

The return clash was set for 3 February 1990 at Vale Park. Of the 20 league games leading up to the fixture, Stoke had only managed four wins and were cast adrift at the bottom of the table, six points from their nearest league neighbour. Vale, the pre-season favourites for relegation, looked to be consolidating their Second Division status, with eight wins between the two derby encounters. The Valiants were on a four-game unbeaten run, winning their previous three, beating Ipswich, West Bromwich Albion and Brighton & Hove Albion prior to the derby. Conversely, Stoke were coming off the back of three straight defeats to Portsmouth, Leeds United and Blackburn Rovers, with relegation looming. The day started where the previous encounters had concluded, with running battles through Burslem town centre, and 35 arrests. Unfortunately, after a bright start, the game petered out into a rather drab affair on an increasingly cut-up pitch, finishing 0-0 in front of the highest home attendance of the season of 22,075.

Though the point was a useful one to Stoke, and they followed it up with a home win against Wolverhampton Wanderers two weeks later, the Potters' form was dire during the run-in, not winning again until the infamous relegation party at the seaside in the final away game at Brighton on 28 April 1990. Most disappointingly for Alan Ball, many of the results during that period from 17 February to 28 April were 0-0 and 1-1 draws, with six one-goal defeats mixed in there too. Despite not winning in 14 consecutive games, only one of those was lost by two or more goals. Then again, even scraping the odd win and extra draw in that run would not have been enough in all likelihood, as Stoke finished bottom on 37 points, 13 adrift of 21st-placed Middlesbrough.

Port Vale's form ebbed and flowed for the remainder of the season following the 0-0 Potteries derby draw, ending the season in a highly respectable 11th place. More importantly, for the first time since before the Second World War, Port Vale were in a higher league than Stoke City – they were the big dogs of the city, at least in league status.

* * *

The two league clashes in the 1989/90 season were a pivotal moment in the history of the Potteries derby. The shared supporters' groups, charitable gestures, generous donations and local well wishes suddenly seemed a distant memory. Ground sharing made way for ground (and town) destroying. The only monetary support would be for the costly police bills. Any opposition fans in the home ends were now either hidden or at risk of expulsion or attack. There would only be one more pre-season friendly between the two sides, in the summer of 1990. Considering the two teams had met practically once a year before that for a friendly or some local cup tie that was essentially a friendly, the abrupt end of the relationship marked a change in attitude and perception between the two sets of supporters, underlined by the 120 arrests across the two Second Division fixtures.

Football fan culture and hooliganism had changed throughout the period where the two clubs were kept apart. The culture had grown through the 1970s and by the late '80s and early '90s, football grounds and the surrounding areas on matchdays had become a hooliganism hotbed, particularly for the likes of Stoke City. No doubt tensions were already running high before and during the two on-field meetings, though premeditated plans of attack were also commonplace. The gradual movement of the two clubs towards each other, and eventual surpassing of league position by Vale, meant that these games were also now on an even keel. They were competitive, tense, unpredictable. The 1950s were far removed for some, and for a new generation, this was the first time the two clubs had met in the league. Of course, it wouldn't be the last. The match had been lit. For Stoke-on-Trent, football in the 1990s was all about the Potteries derbies, and it was about to hit its peak.

5

Stuck in the Mud

OK, THIS should be a good chapter.

By the 1992/93 season, both Stoke-on-Trent teams were back in the newly christened Second Division, the third tier now renamed as part of the new structural branding of the English league system, from the Premier League downwards. After a couple of early losses, the rivals began to gather momentum through September and October, heading for the first Potteries derby of the season on 24 October 1992 at the Victoria Ground. Stoke were at the start of what would turn out to be an incredible league run between 5 September 1992 and 20 February 1993, led by the goal machine and 'Golden One', Mark Stein. The centre-forward was already within a couple of goals of double figures for the season, well on his way to a remarkable 33 in all competitions, including 26 in the league, for the whole campaign. Vale were also benefitting from a glut of early season goals, but theirs were predominantly shared between Ian Taylor, Paul Kerr, Nicky Cross and Martin Foyle.

The 1992/93 season was set to be an iconic one for the two Potteries teams for many reasons, not least the two men in the respective dugouts. In the red and white corner, often sporting a cosy LM-marked red Stoke City jumper, was Manchester United and Scotland legend Lou Macari. In the black and white corner, sporting a *Peaky Blinders*-style flat black cap and, in oft-typical cold and rainy Potteries weather conditions, long, dark overcoat, John Rudge, ever-present at the club since his appointment to the hot seat in 1983. Two celebrated managers, and two locally famous teams.

Many of the players from both squads are well regarded to this day – I say well regarded, not so much from the opposing fans, I guess. Port Vale fans still bring out the song 'Steino is a t*sser, he wears a t*sser's hat, he plays for the City, he is a f*cking tw*t, he dives down the left wing, he dives down the right, he couldn't score a goal if he played all f*cking night'. It's a colourful chant born out of the events of this very 1992/93 season, and the ill feeling has lasted to this day.

Speaking of such sassy chants, the two managers wouldn't long be free of such treatment from their opposition rivals. The response to the old Manchester United (and newly adopted Stoke City) chant of 'Lou, Lou skip to my Lou, skip to my Lou Macari' would of course become 'sh*t on Lou Macari', while Rudge would receive, among others, 'Johnny Rudge is illegitimate, he ain't got no birth certificate, he's a Vale b*stard'. Arnold Bennett would be proud.

Anyway, back to the league and the build-up to the October meeting. Both clubs were looking to jump up into the play-offs, and possibly the automatic promotion places. The home side Stoke were coming off two straight wins and were unbeaten in eight. The visitors were coming off four straight wins, unbeaten in seven.

Something had to give. A capacity crowd of 24,459 packed into the famous old ground, with tensions typically high throughout the day. Scarves were held aloft as the players emerged from the dressing rooms from both sets of fans, both knitted with the claim of being 'The Pride of the Potteries'. Stoke were sporting their famous red-and-white-striped kit, with a little flash of black on the sides and collar and 'ANSELLS' sprawled across the middle, white shorts and red socks, while Vale were in an all-yellow strip with similar black trimmings and 'KALAMAZOO' tapering out like something from the cover of a comic book. As the game started, Vale keeper Paul Musselwhite was busy keeping out the predator Stein as Stoke piled on the early pressure. It settled down after 20 minutes with the visitors sitting in and making it hard work for the home side to create chances in the first half. After the break things opened up, and the visitors took the lead in the 67th minute when Paul Kerr converted an Ian Taylor pass with a curling effort to send the away end into ecstasy. Fans at the front climbed the red fences as Kerr and co wheeled away in celebration. Not a minute later, the score was levelled as Stoke substitute Kevin 'Rooster' Russell sent a free kick towards the back post, where central defender Ian Cranson powered his header into the roof of the net, and it was the home fans' turn to celebrate and taunt.

The outcome was decided four minutes from time when Stein beat the offside trap before being brought down in the box by Musselwhite. The decision was a controversial one, diplomatically described by *The Sentinel* as 'there was contact, however minimal'. Stein picked up the ball to take it himself, with the words of Vale defender Peter Swan ringing in his ear, 'Let's see how your bottle is.' After several minutes of protest and being kept waiting, the 'Golden One' rifled the spot kick into the bottom-right corner, before being mobbed by his team-mates as fans spilled on to the pitch to celebrate with the players.

Later recalling the incident, Stein said, 'Swanny obviously gave me a bit of abuse and said something like, "Let's see how your bottle is." But I never felt any nerves at all. I was confident I was going to score. The referee actually kept me waiting and I knew the importance of it and knew it was in the last five minutes. But I never had any doubt I was going to score. People still ask me now if it was a penalty, but Musselwhite made a mistake coming out thinking he could get it and the fact they tried to claim he didn't was embarrassing really – but it was such a big game.'

A few minutes later, the referee blew the final whistle and several hundred Stoke fans climbed the advertising boards and piled on to the pitch to celebrate with the team, and of course, to taunt the away end. Police and stewards moved quickly to form a barrier to prevent the two sets of fans getting too close, with horses and dogs deployed to disperse the encroachers. The Vale fans were kept behind while order was restored, and the home fans left the field and the stands with cheers of jubilation. Winning the Potteries derby simply meant everything.

Describing the lead-up to the game, Stein recounted, 'I remember walking over Campbell Road and the atmosphere was electric. We could feel it. Lou never used to want us to get there too early. We'd get there for 2pm. He thought the later we could get changed, the less nervous we'd get. But I remember that day, you could hear the noise coming through the windows of the changing room. There was this hissing sound. The ground was packed solid, and that noise was like something I had never known. I'd had derbies before for Luton against Watford, but Stoke–Vale was something different. Two really good teams challenging for promotion, and we all knew what it meant. Lou didn't have to stoke it up, he knew as much as us that we needed to turn them over.'

The penalty incident has become a matter of fact for fans on both sides. Ally Simcock recalled moments as a Vale supporter coming up against Stein both during his playing career and after, jesting, 'Mark Stein had a lot to answer for. I remember meeting him years later at Barnet and he was a really nice bloke with a wicked sense of humour. But I'm afraid I can't forgive him!' By contrast, KnotFM presenter and Stoke City Fans Council member Angela Smith recounted, 'It was two days before my mum's birthday, she was as big a Stoke fan as me, and desperate for a win to start off the birthday celebrations. This game did not disappoint. Both teams were doing well, and it was a tight game, but with a few minutes left, Steino beat the offside trap and Musselwhite came out of goal and brought him down. If VAR had been around, it would have confirmed the decision however much the Vale fans protested. Funnily enough, Steino had missed a penalty a couple of weeks before but that meant nothing. He placed the ball into the corner of the net and the Boothen End went mad.' *The Sentinel*'s Stoke City reporter Pete Smith is defiant in his statement, 'Stein definitely didn't dive, and I would defend him to the hilt.'

With the win, Stoke moved up to fourth, and their winning streak and unbeaten run rolled on. Vale bounced back quickly with back-to-back victories and an unbeaten stretch of their own. The day ended with 24 arrests, any number of them in Hanley that night. If the authorities were not aware of the bad blood between the two sets of fans and were caught slightly off-guard before the two meetings in 1989/90, they were certainly ready by 1992. They had to be, because less than a month later, the two teams would meet again.

* * *

Both teams continued to impress with their league form in the run-up to the next Potteries derby on 16 November 1992, this time an FA Cup first round clash at the Victoria Ground. Naturally, for such a spicy first round fixture, the game was selected for coverage by the fledgling satellite broadcaster Sky Sports, which meant dancing cheerleaders before kick-off, fireworks to greet the emerging players, and even a giant sumo wrestling competition at half-time!

The pomp and circumstance did give the event a more colourful, carnival feel, but tensions in the sold-out ground were high, and the Valiants were still sore after losing to the late penalty the previous month. Vale were backed by a massive 6,700 fans for the cup clash, but they would have been forgiven for fearing the tie was going to go the way of the home side after a first-half showing that included six Stoke corners in the opening 20 minutes. Vale remained resolute and weathered the storm then came out stronger in the second half. Stein and Nigel Gleghorn went close to opening the scoring for the home side, while Taylor and Foyle had Vale's best efforts. The game ended 0-0, meaning a replay and an extra fixture for the two sides battling for promotion in the league.

The replay at Vale Park was set for 24 November 1992, and it would become a famous (or infamous) night, one of the most memorable meetings between the two sides. By late November, Stoke were sitting pretty at the top of the Second Division league table, while Vale were making good progress too, occupying fifth place. Not for the first, or last time, events in and around the stadium were troubling, with Stoke fans wrecking the Ye Olde Crown pub before the match, causing an estimated £20,000 of damage. The Hamil

End, where the Stoke fans were situated, would also get the same treatment, with £5,000 of damage caused. On the evening, the conditions were biblical as the rain lashed down in Burslem and the pitch was left looking like a place more fitting of the nearby Dimensions swimming centre rather than a football match. Before the game, Port Vale manager John Rudge described the pitch as 'a bit sticky'. The replay was again broadcast live on Sky, with the events preserved on tape for years to come on various *FA Cup Years* replays, which must be wonderful for one set of supporters.

The match was a hard-hitting affair. As well as fan clashes and team hostilities, there were individual battles waging too. Port Vale defender Neil Aspin went up against Stoke midfielder Steve Foley in the first 15 minutes, at which point the personal contest was abruptly ended as Foley went in hard and over the ball on the centre-half. Aspin would end up in hospital with a knee injury, while Foley was lucky to escape punishment from the referee. Recalling the incident, Aspin would later say, 'I suppose you realise in the game that it was a bad challenge. But I had never actually seen the incident again until last year [2016], but I remember speaking to a knee specialist and he said he didn't know how my knee didn't snap. When I watched it last year, I realised I was very fortunate, I don't know how I got away with that one. The biggest regret is I never got the chance to return the favour! I never got the opportunity in my career, but I would have liked to have been able to play against him again. It was one of the most blatant red cards you could see, but I played again within a few weeks, so it wasn't as bad as it probably looked at the time.'

Looking back on match reports, I saw in *The Sentinel* this remark on the tackle, 'It wasn't a red card … it was a prison sentence!'

The game continued as the pouring rain refused to relent. It was the visitors that took the lead after 23 minutes. A Russell free kick into the Vale box was headed towards goal by Vince Overson, but it was fellow defender Lee Sandford who would prod home from a couple of yards out in the muddy six-yard box to give Stoke the advantage. A few stray arms were flung up in celebration in the home end behind the goal, quickly self-withdrawn or muted by those around them.

Stoke had taken the lead, but this time it was Vale's turn to hit back immediately. Some 90 seconds later the two Stoke central defenders got into a mix-up at the back, allowing Martin Foyle to go through on goal and slide past Ronnie Sinclair into the bottom corner in front of the away fans. As Andy Porter jumped on Foyle's back to celebrate, he couldn't resist ribbing his team-mate by declaring 'offside!' in the striker's ear.

Before the break, the home side took the lead, as Ray Walker's forward ball was met by the head of Porter, playing in Nicky Cross, who knocked the ball back down into Porter's path to rifle home an unstoppable finish from 18 yards. Vale fans spilled on to the river-like track by the side of the pitch in celebration following the strike. Vale led 2-1 at the break. It was an important goal as giving them the half-time advantage probably kept the tie from being abandoned due to the monsoon conditions and waterlogged pitch. Perhaps the game being on Sky also kept the players out on the pitch too, as Foyle would later say, 'If it wasn't a local derby and if it wasn't on Sky TV, the game would have been called off, there's no question about that. It was hazardous.'

The decision to continue was soon looking suspect, at least in the eyes of Stoke City supporters, as perhaps the defining images of all Potteries derbies played out in the second half. Fresh off the bench for the Potters, Dave Regis immediately got into the game, steering the ball to Stein who played a forward pass. Musselwhite came rampaging out of his box to meet the ball, but under pressure could only miscue it into Regis's path, some 23 yards out, directly in front of the open goal. Regis immediately steered the ball goalwards as the Stoke fans behind the net began to cheer. Then, around the penalty spot, the ball got stuck in the mud, before coming to a stop six yards from the line. The penalty box was essentially a pond and Regis, possibly not quite acclimatised to the conditions, simply didn't hit the ball hard enough to reach the goal.

The Vale players had certainly adapted, playing balls forward that would ordinarily roll through to the keeper or out into touch for a throw-in or goal kick. Not on this night though. Foyle would go close with a header, while a volley from Regis from eight yards out somehow ended up closer to the centre circle. With a few minutes remaining Taylor was presented with a chance to make it 3-1 to the home side, but somehow prodded wide from around the penalty spot with only Sinclair to beat.

With Stoke committing men forward, Vale were looking the more likely to score the fourth goal of the game on the break. John Jeffers and Foyle both spurned golden chances, before in the final seconds, Cross once again made best use of the conditions to play a long ball forward that stuck in the mud, allowing Foyle to round the advancing Sinclair and prod the ball (with a little more force and air on it than Regis's effort) into the empty net. Vale fans spilled on to the pitch, and a classic encounter ended 3-1 to the home side in front of 19,810. No doubt a few pairs of muddy trainers and jeans went in the washing machines of Burslem and

Tunstall that night. The Port Vale fans were singing in the rain.

After the battle in the mud, Lou Macari was not too downbeat in defeat, saying, 'I would not criticise any of my players for this result. I thought they battled magnificently, and the outcome was scant reward for all the hard work they put in. They probably worked harder than any Stoke team has done for years.' John Rudge was also diplomatic in victory, stating, 'Stoke are a good team and we had to match them in every quarter. I hope we will be together at the top of the table at the end of the season.'

Aspin recalled, 'I had to go to hospital to get checked, but at least while I was waiting, I was able to watch the game on the screen. It was a fantastic night. A great atmosphere, and I still remember the ball sticking in the mud.'

My Vale-supporting mate Patrick Floyd looked back, 'I always remember Regis taking that shot, and it was going in, then it just stopped. Then later on, Foyle did the same, but being the superior player, he got it over the mud and in! I remember watching the crowd, I've never seen a Vale Park crowd like that – it was heaving. You don't see it like that anymore.'

Ally Simcock also pinpointed the prominent cup tie as a personal highlight, 'One of my most favourite memories was the FA Cup victory which was complete with a "stuck in the mud" moment. Dave Regis struck the ball, and it was on target ... but the mud put paid to that. Stoke may have beaten us home and away that season but I'll never forget the joy on Vale's faces when they snatched victory in the cup!'

The Sky Sports coverage was summed up nicely when Martin Tyler professionally stated that he was sorry for the fans watching football in such poor conditions, while his long-standing summariser Andy Gray simply retorted, 'Nah Martin, these are real fans ... they love it.'

* * *

The FA Cup first round replay became a legendary match in the staggered history between the two clubs. The conditions played into the occasion in a dramatic manner. The game had stunning goals, tough tackles, exciting incidents and tense drama right to the end, played out by two on-fire teams who detested each other, led by two managers that were in the middle of forging their lasting reputations, surrounded by TV cameras and a ferocious atmosphere that boiled over on several occasions.

The Potters weren't used to tasting defeat at that time, so the infliction of such a theatrical loss would have been a bitter pill to swallow, and the team needed to bounce back quickly to sustain their promotion bid. After a couple of draws, Vale were hoping that the morale-boosting win would provide a bounce in the league, as the Valiants were playing catch-up in the chasing pack just behind table-toppers Stoke. As Christmas 1992 came around, heading into 1993, we had something that generations of Potteries football fans had never seen, and perhaps would never see again: a legitimate promotion challenge, starring Stoke City and Port Vale.

Oh, and the two teams weren't done in cup competitions either.

6

Trophy Hunters

AS 1993 rolled around, Stoke City were on fire. The Potters hadn't lost a league game since 2 September 1992, a run which would continue all the way up to 27 February 1993. A massive 25-match unbeaten streak, with 17 wins (including seven in a row), was finally ended with a 1-0 defeat at Leyton Orient. Mark Stein had gone into goalscoring overdrive, backed up by Foley, Regis, Russell and Shaw, supported from midfield by Gleghorn, Beeston and Ware, and with crucial contributions from defenders Sandford, Cranson and Butler.

Since the FA Cup win against Stoke, Vale had also kicked on through to the new year with only one defeat up to 13 February 1993, including six victories on the bounce. Two defeats in mid-February meant the Valiants' chasing-down of table-toppers Stoke was slightly stunted, leaving them seven points behind their neighbours, but both teams were in prime position for an unprecedented Stoke-on-Trent promotion double.

Before reaching the crucial run-in, and all-important return league fixture at Vale Park, the two teams would meet in cup competition once again, meaning there would be an extraordinary five head-to-heads across 1992/93. This time it was in the Autoglass Trophy, aka the EFL Trophy. Since its inception in 1984 the annual competition has generally only been open to clubs in the bottom two divisions in the Football League, with the occasional invited National League team involved (prior to the controversial introduction of upper-league academies/under-21 sides from the latter years of the 2010s). While the cup has historically been seen as a very low priority, often providing a run out for fringe and youth players in front of modest crowds, it does provide perennial lower league clubs starved of success with a chance to win a trophy (or for a period of time, a massive shield), and offers a big day out to Wembley Stadium (or for a period of time, the Millennium Stadium). As a result, attendances usually go up and starting 11s are strengthened by the time the semi-finals and final roll around. For more reputable teams that have slid down the divisions, it provides a chance to flex their supportive muscles on final day, with up to 40,000 tickets potentially made available for each team. Because the initial rounds are split up into northern and southern sections, there is an increased likelihood of meeting a local rival, as was the case on a few occasions with Stoke and Vale (more to come). It can also add an extra song to a fanbase's repertoire, such as Stoke's own 'The Autoglass Trophy, we've won it two times', sung tongue-in-cheek during the Premier League years at places like Anfield and Old Trafford. The song would normally be followed by someone yelling 'Have you ever won it? Have you f*ck!' towards the bewildered home fans and day-trippers.

The first of Stoke's two prestigious Autoglass Trophy wins came in the 1991/92 season, so the Potters were the holders at the time of the Vale clash. Their 16 May 1992 1-0 win against Stockport County at Wembley Stadium in front of 48,339 was a huge occasion for the Potters with the winner coming from Stein. Stockport weren't particularly liked at the time, which added to the occasion. For many people, it was their first experience of Wembley as a Stoke fan, the first time in such a big travelling crowd and the first taste of silverware. Painted faces, jester hats, open-top buses – for a competition that is generally looked down upon, it can sure provide some memorable moments.

Stoke and Vale found themselves in the southern section in 1992/93 (still don't know where Stoke-on-Trent belongs). Stoke had seen off Wrexham, Crewe Alexandra, Barnet and West Bromwich Albion on their way to the southern section semi-final. After not needing to go through the preliminary rounds, Vale saw their way past Fulham and Northampton to set up the Autoglass Potteries derby with the holders.

Another bumper Victoria Ground crowd of 22,267 was in attendance for the next chapter of this never-ending tussle between the two teams. Both clubs fielded their strongest 11s, as Stoke looked to avenge their defeat in the FA Cup, while Vale were looking for their first competitive win at the Victoria Ground since 1927. Stoke came out firing in the first half, putting pressure on the Vale goal from the off, with Stein missing a series of chances. On 12 minutes Taylor tripped Shaw in the box to once again present Stein with the chance from the penalty spot to put Stoke ahead against Vale at the Vic. However, his tame effort could only rattle the post, to the shock of the majority in attendance.

Stoke continued to sustain the pressure, and Vale lost Martin Foyle to injury just before half-time. Beeston went close for Stoke with a spectacular 45-yard lob, and Stein eventually did find the net, but it was ruled out for offside. The yellow wall managed to hold on until the break and the Valiants regrouped. The half-time message from Lou Macari was most likely 'more of the same please'. John Rudge's approach was to throw down the challenge to his team, 'This is going to be our night. How badly do you want it?'

The rallying call from the visiting manager did the trick as Vale came out firing in the second half, and took the lead thanks to Robin van der Laan. The popular Dutchman, who had arrived in Burslem in 1991, got his head on a Chris Sully free kick which van der Laan had himself won, beating Ronnie Sinclair at his right-hand post in front of the travelling support. Van der Laan slid on his knees to celebrate with the fans, who were again clambering on the railings under the Victoria Ground floodlights.

Stoke once again came back firing but this time there was no immediate response. Stein, the Potters' man of the moment, must have packed the wrong boots on the evening as he spurned two more gilt-edged chances to bring the home side level. Paul Musselwhite was also in inspired form, again keeping out Beeston and withstanding wave after wave of attack. In the end one goal was enough, as Stoke's ten attempts, including the penalty, couldn't beat the Vale number one, while the visitors needed only two shots on goal to do the job.

At the final whistle, Rudge, in his flat cap and buttoned-up overcoat, threw his fist in the air in the direction of the jubilant travelling Valeites as Port Vale registered their first victory at Stoke in a competitive match since the 1920s. The Vale manager reflected, 'We did not play as well as we would have liked but we got the result we wanted. We had to battle for it, and we defended exceptionally well. On the night we had that little bit of the rub of the green; one or two things went for us like the penalty miss, but we had to work hard. When you think of all the things that have gone against us – we only had 13 fit players and then we lose Martin Foyle – to have beaten Stoke on their own patch is a magnificent achievement.'

The victory at the Vic, now the Valiants' second win of the season against their bitter rivals, put to bed any lingering feeling of inferiority. Separated by just one position at the very top of the league, with two wins, a draw and a defeat from the four meetings, and with a realistic chance of winning two trophies, Vale were on top of the world again. Rudge's men would go on to beat Exeter City 3-2 over two legs in the southern section final, setting up a final with Stockport, at Wembley for a second year running in the competition. But before that there was still everything to play for in the promotion chase, and another meeting with the league leaders Stoke City at Vale Park.

* * *

After a few poor results at the back end of February and start of March, both teams recovered with back-to-back wins before Vale made it three in a row with a victory at Hull, while Stoke were beaten at home by struggling Blackpool on 27 March 1993, their first home league defeat of the season. The gap at the top was still seven points, but the surprise home defeat for the Potters, coupled with the recent cup victories for the Valiants, added even more fuel to the fiery league clash at Vale Park on 31 March. Once again the attendance shot up to an all-ticket 20,373, up from 7,747 in the previous home game, for what was seen as the most highly anticipated league clash between the two sides in living memory. Victory for Stoke would all but seal automatic promotion to the First Division, but a win for Vale would mount the pressure on the leaders going into the final stage of the season. A four-point lead for Stoke would look a lot more perilous than ten points, especially with tough trips ahead to the likes of Stockport, Huddersfield and promotion-chasing Bolton Wanderers.

The home side were without their talismanic midfielder Ian Taylor, while there was a rare outing in the Stoke goal for serial league championship, European Cup and domestic cup winner Bruce Grobbelaar, loaned out from Liverpool in the second half of the season. The somewhat unpredictable Grobbelaar was replacing the injured Ronnie Sinclair, who was out for the rest of the campaign. Otherwise, the teams lined up with the players who had brought them to the dance.

The rain was once again hammering down on a cold Wednesday night, and the pitch was still sporting the same brown muddy scars that had plagued Stoke before, but it wasn't quite the swamp conditions of the FA Cup. There were once again pre-match fireworks, though they weren't organised Sky TV pyrotechnics, but red smoke bombs from the away end, again shrouding ST6 1AW in an ominous dispersed mist. For the travelling Stoke fans a match ticket was like gold dust, with more than a few taking up tickets in the home end. My own mum and dad had somehow wangled tickets in the home end too. A bit of crafty dealing on my dad's part saw him score two tickets side by side in the Railway Stand. Well, not *exactly* side by side. While the tickets were numerically next to each other, they were in fact on either side of the stairway in the home end. A few sage words of advice from my dad to my mum across the stairs on the night, 'Now Kath, remember we're in enemy territory here, so try to keep your mouth shut, and don't cheer if we score!'

* * *

As the game got under way, there were immediate fouls given away by both teams. The Vale fans were booing Stein's every touch after the penalty controversy at the Vic. Stein had also missed a glut of chances in the Autoglass Trophy clash. Each miss this time was met with ironic 'AAAAH' shouts from the crowd. These days, fans give it the big comical 'WHEEEY' when an opposition player misses or kicks it in to touch. It's kind of a shame; I kind of like the old 'AAAAH' shouts.

While the lawfulness of Stein's goal earlier in the season was debated, there was no doubt about the validity and quality of his effort after five minutes to open the scoring at Vale Park. John Butler powered down the right wing, crossing to the Stoke hitman to strike a crisp half-volley past Musselwhite to send the packed away end of some 7,200 Potters behind the goal into a frenzy. It was the kind of classic 'mental' celebration that crops up on Twitter every few months, as a sea of fans bounce and seemingly move like a wave crashing into the coastline. Oh, and of course my mum celebrated in the home end too. 'Sh*t's in! Sh*t's in the home end!' were the cries from the Vale fans towards my mum. My dad bravely stood up to say, 'Look, we're just here to watch the match! We don't want any bother,' before shooting a sharp eye at my dear mother. My parents were probably fortunate to get away with a barrage of verbal abuse rather than anything physical; they were possibly saved by other fans celebrating in the home end too.

The goal settled any nerves that Stein may have been harbouring from the Autoglass Trophy game, showing some sublime footwork to create space in the box and cause more problems for the Vale back line. As the first half progressed the home side came back into the game, led by their recent signing Bernie Slaven. His trickery and determination forced a tidy save from Grobbelaar just before half-time, but it was Stoke who went in at the break with the lead. As the second half got under way, the intensity of the match was too much for some and referee Roger Milford limped off, substituted for his senior linesman after a collision with Ray Walker and picking up a muscle strain.

The visitors in red and white were beginning to rise to the occasion once again though, with Dave Regis experiencing better fortunes than on his previous visit to Vale Park, winning a free kick that Nigel Gleghorn struck well, but the shot was thwarted by the diving Musselwhite. 'Foghorn' Gleghorn wasn't to be denied for long though, heading home a Dave Kevan corner after 64 minutes, beating the defender on the line by just a few inches to creep in between man and bar. Stoke were now fully in control, with Stein testing the palms of Musselwhite after some good link-up play with Regis.

With time running out the Valiants made one last push to grab a goal and mount late pressure, but

Grobbelaar did magnificently to keep out Slaven's dipping effort from outside the area. In the end Stoke picked up the all-important win, going ten points clear at the top, promotion all but sealed. Grobbelaar turned to both celebrate with the fans and implore them to keep off the pitch, which, to their credit, they did. The day ended with 25 arrests, a number that was actually pleasing to the police, given the importance of the fixture. Angela Smith gave her recollection of her night behind the goal: 'We were flying, and tickets were like gold dust. What an atmosphere in the away end. Steino again scored a belter of a volley after Butler had burst down the wing to set him up. It was great for Stein because earlier that month he had missed a bucketful of chances against them in the Autoglass. To make it even better, the goal went in at the end that we were all packed into. Gleghorn got the second and that win put Stoke ten points clear. We never looked back after that game in that season.'

The hero of the red and white side of the city, Stein, recounted, 'It was one of my favourite goals. We'd played them earlier that month in the Autoglass and I'd missed all those chances and I took a load of stick from their supporters. But that game at Vale Park was a defining moment. It was a massive game and I remember scoring at that end which was just full of thousands of Stoke supporters and sending them crazy.

We played really well that night. I remember coming off and in the changing room we all knew what a big night it was for us and that probably actually sealed us getting promotion. We were ten points clear, and we knew we weren't going to make the same mistakes we did the year before. It made it really special.'

Stein was referring to the previous season's play-off defeat at the hands of Stockport, after the Potters had staggered through their final few league game, to finish fourth. Lou Macari also had the exorcism of the previous year on his mind in his post-match thoughts: 'We're better than last year. When we lost on Saturday, people were starting to say, "Are they going to do what they did last year?" I've never felt like we've got the sort of team that will panic like we did last year. I'm confident we can last the pace.' When quizzed on whether Stoke were now out of reach, John Rudge responded, 'We want to finish in the first or second spot, we'd be quite happy with that. I said before tonight's match that I didn't think Stoke would finish anywhere other than the first or second spot. It's the Boltons, the West Broms and the Stockports that I'm a little bit more concerned about. We want to go for promotion in first or second spot.'

Both 1992/93 meetings at Vale Park were highly memorable clashes, and the fact that they were both captured by the TV cameras means that fans can relive them over and over again. For the league clash, the match was the focus of a *Central Sports Special*, with none other than England legend Jimmy Greaves providing the analysis. He referred to Butler's run down the right for Stein's opener as showing 'shades of Sir Stanley in the old red and white'. Although after being full of praise for Port Vale's season and performance, Greavsie snuck in a cheeky comment of, 'Not many people know where Port Vale is, I've never been … thank God!' To be fair, he did add, 'Good luck to them, I hope they come up.' Both 20-minute highlight, packages are available on YouTube, so go out of your way to watch the one that fits your own supportive needs.

YouTube isn't always the best place to find high-quality highlights for old Stoke or Vale games (one Port Vale highlights package that I found seemed to be 75 per cent still photographs of Steed Malbranque playing against the Valiants for Spurs, to the tune of Billy Joel's classic 'We Didn't Start the Fire'), but the full match coverage through fan sites onevalefan and PortValeOnline have been a great resource to me.

* * *

The remaining job for Lou Macari's men was to not spectacularly collapse and blow their head start in the final nine games of the season. Promotion was highly likely; going up as champions was the ultimate goal. The two games that followed the Potteries derby ramped up the tension, with Stoke only taking one point from the two tricky away games at Stockport and Huddersfield. However, back-to-back wins followed, and despite a home slip-up against Hartlepool, by the 28 April 1993 home game with Plymouth Argyle Stoke were one win away from sealing promotion.

The evening game started with Peter Fox, now back deputising in goal, pulling off some early heroics to keep out a point-blank header, before somehow reaching the follow-up to keep the game goalless. Barely a minute later, Stoke went ahead thanks to Gleghorn, smashing in from six yards out after clever play from Graham Shaw. The Vic was bouncing as the fans sensed a romp to seal promotion in style. It didn't play out that way, though, as the game became a tense affair, with Fox even turning to the Boothen End to try to calm down the nervy supporters. Stoke were forced to defend resolutely, with Overson throwing himself in front of everything, eventually requiring three stitches and a headband to see out the final minutes of the game. As Stoke fans gathered at the front of the stands ready to invade the pitch, Fox once again kept his cool, preventing a late equaliser from a deflected shot. 'Foxy' was the hero of the day as the full-time whistle blew, and the Victoria Ground stands emptied with fans piling on to the pitch to celebrate. Stoke had secured the Second Division title with two games to spare. The players emerged from the sea of supporters to join in the party from atop the Boothen Stand balcony. As *The Sentinel*'s Stoke reporter at the time, Ian Bayley, summed up, 'On the night it wasn't a vintage performance, but championships are won over nine months and, on that score, no one can dispute Stoke City the trophy.'

With top spot sealed by their local rivals, Port Vale were, and in truth had been for several weeks, battling it out for second spot with Bolton Wanderers, West Brom and Stockport. The Valiants' recovery from the Potteries derby defeat, with two wins and a draw from the next three, meant they were still looking good for promotion. However, Bolton were also hitting their own white-hot form, and with the Lancastrians and the boys from Burslem both winning three in a row it would be a question of who would blink first with two games to go. Unfortunately for Vale, they could only manage a 1-1 draw away to Exeter on 4 May 1993, meaning they needed good news from Bolton and a favour from their opponents. The opposition on that day? None other than the already crowned champions, Stoke City.

It wouldn't come as a big surprise to learn that the Stoke players weren't exactly 100 per cent prepared and committed to the task of stopping Wanderers. Ian Cranson would recall, 'I remember the relief after the [Plymouth] game and then the celebration. We went into Newcastle and [director] Bob Kenyon bought us a few drinks. The biggest thing was Lou saying before that if we win, we go up as champions and he didn't want to see us again until the end of the season. It was a case of if we had won, we could just turn up for the remaining matches. That was the incentive! So, we did, and then there was Bolton away, Burnley at home left. We planned to travel up to Bolton on the day of the game and it was almost just, "See you on the bus!" Lou said to us, "You've done it, other clubs can't expect you to do them any favours, so go and enjoy it." We had a two- or three-day gap when we didn't train, then Chic Bates got us in on the morning of the game and that was it. I think ultimately by Bolton beating us they forced Vale out of the top two. But we had done it, we had worked hard. We had done our job.'

Automatic promotion wasn't to be for Port Vale that season. Stoke went down 1-0 to Bolton, who wrapped up their season with a 1-0 win at home to Preston to seal second spot. The Potters celebrated their championship win with a 1-1 draw at home to Burnley, while Vale picked up some much-needed momentum heading into the play-offs with a 4-2 victory at Blackpool. The mood at Vale Park was anything but gloomy, though. They now had three straight games against Stockport County to look forward to – two in the play-offs, and one in the Autoglass Trophy Final.

The play-off semi-finals were first up. It was Stockport, who had finished 17 points behind Vale in the league, who took an early lead at Edgeley Park thanks to a penalty converted by future Vale manager Jim Gannon. Dean Glover equalised for the visitors with a header, meaning Vale would go into the second leg on level terms. The return fixture was a few days later on 19 May, in front of 12,689 at Vale Park. It was a closely contested encounter, with Stockport goalkeeper Neil Edwards called into action on several occasions to keep out Paul Kerr and Ian Taylor, as the visitors looked to strike with long balls and Mike Flynn's long throws. Perhaps the presence of their absent 6ft 7in forward Kevin Francis would have made a difference, but it was Martin Foyle who eventually settled the tie six minutes from time. The Vale front man caught Bernie Slaven's cross on the half-volley to finally beat Edwards. The goal was enough to seal the 2-1 aggregate victory and book another trip to Wembley for the Valiants. The club had waited 117 years for a trip to the national stadium – now they had two trips in eight days.

The city of Stoke-on-Trent was still buzzing from the Potters' championship win, the play-off victory for the Valiants and a season of five dramatic Potteries derbies. It wouldn't be long before a second trophy of the season was brought back to the Potteries, this time for Port Vale. It was a proud occasion for John Rudge to lead his team out at the famous old stadium, ten years into his tenure in the hot seat and on his first trip to Wembley too. The Valiants ran out 2-1 winners in the Autoglass Trophy Final against the hapless Stockport (three Wembley defeats in just over a year for the Hatters), thanks to first-half goals from Paul Kerr and Bernie Slaven, in front of 35,885 at Wembley on 22 May, more than 28,000 supporting the Vale.

The Valiants dominated the first half, and their two-goal lead at the break was more than justified. The giant Francis pulled one back for County, setting up a tense finale, but Port Vale hung on for victory. It was the turn of the northern half of the city to celebrate a trophy by packing the streets clad in bucket hats, flags and scarves, with a sea of black, white and yellow celebrating in the capital, and again the next day for the homecoming parade. The 'WELCOME TO STOKE ON TRENT' street sign in Goldenhill had been changed to 'VALE ON TRENT', as the open-top yellow and white PMT bus toured the black and white hotspots of the city, inevitably finishing up in Burslem's main Market Square. One pub landlord spelled out a clear message to the team with a banner reading 'Well done the Vale. Halfway to paradise'. Play-off final success against West Bromwich Albion was the next and final target.

The Valiants would be outnumbered by their West Midlands counterparts on 30 May, but they were hoping not to be outgunned on the pitch. Vale started quite nervously, however, as a miskick from Musselwhite presented the Baggies with the first meaningful chance of the game, but Kevin Donovan put his effort wide with only the goalkeeper to beat. Another nervy moment for the Vale number one came when a long, hopeful ball forward almost caught him out, slipping near the edge of his area but managing to hold the bouncing ball and preventing it from looping over him. The first half ended 0-0, with Vale growing into the game before the interval mainly thanks to the tidy build-up play of Slaven.

Albion came out strongly in the second half, Donovan again unable to find the net after being played through on goal and only managing to hit a tame shot into the grateful clutches of Musselwhite. Ian Taylor's deep cross almost caught out West Brom goalkeeper Tony Lange, who tipped the dipping ball over the bar for a corner. The closely contested game would turn on the hour, though, as a long ball forward from Ian Hamilton caught the Vale back line flat-footed, allowing Albion's legendary forward Bob Taylor a free run on goal. Just as Taylor carried the ball into the semi-circle on the edge of the box, Vale defender Peter Swan came in on the striker from behind, getting nothing on the ball but clearing out the man. Swan sheepishly got to hit feet as the free kick was awarded and approached the referee. Roger Milford, who had limped off during the Potteries derby league clash at Vale Park earlier in the season, calmly took out his book, said a few words, and eventually brandished his red card. Swan's fate was sealed, and not long after, Vale's fate was sealed too. Albion were in front seven minutes later thanks to Andy Hunt's looping header. Late goals from Nicky Reid and Kevin Donovan piled on the misery for Vale, as Ossie Ardiles's team booked their place in the First Division. The Valiants had finally run out of steam after a gruelling 61-game season.

After such a wonderful campaign, it was a bitter pill to swallow for John Rudge and Port Vale. Rudge said after the play-off defeat, 'You can't ask much more of a team than to get 89 points, which would have won us the championship last year. It's a cruel game.' In the end, after 46 league games, four FA Cup ties and two in the League Cup, a further six Autoglass Trophy games and then the three play-off fixtures, the Port Vale tank was empty.

It was still a history-making, hugely successful season for the Valiants though, who tasted silverware and Wembley victory for the first time in their history, grabbed their first win at the Victoria Ground since 1927, overcame Stoke in two cup competitions and racked up a mightily impressive 89 points in the league. But 1992/93 belonged to Stoke City. Despite the two cup defeats, the two Potteries derby league wins were critical in their relentless charge to the title, with an absolutely stunning 25-game unbeaten run granting Lou Macari and his team, led up top by Mark Stein, hero status among Stoke fans secured for years to come.

Pete Smith recounted his memories of that memorable season, 'I was nine turning ten, when you really start falling in love with football, in the 1992/93 season, so those matches, the atmospheres and that fierce competitiveness stayed with me. There were great, intense rivalries with West Brom and Stockport, but nothing touched this for the best part of a decade. Each game was a blockbuster with leading men: Stein, Gleghorn, Cranson, van der Laan, Ian Taylor, Aspin, as well as two brilliant managers. I probably didn't realise at the time just how tribal it all was. Stoke's win at Vale Park in late March 1993 pretty much sealed promotion, and everyone knew it. It was a beautifully taken goal from Stein after a great run from John Butler and the away end just wasn't big enough to contain the Stoke fans. It was the perfect identity for a Stoke team, skilful but tough and strong.'

The 1992/93 season was like no other for football in Stoke-on-Trent. What a story. Five derby games across three competitions, Port Vale coming out on top in the two cup encounters in dramatic fashion and Stoke coming out on top in the league, with the Potters' late-season defeat to Bolton meaning Vale missed out on automatic promotion too. Plenty of arrests, huge crowds, TV cameras, dancers, entertainers, and a stagnant ball in the middle of a puddle of mud. Stoke moved one division ahead of Vale but it wouldn't be for long. The 1990s were far from finished with the Potteries derby.

7

Victoria Falls

PORT VALE would follow in Stoke City's footsteps in 1993/94 by going one better than their previous promotion attempt the very next season. The Valiants were promoted automatically, taking second place thanks to five wins from their last five games, with Martin Foyle finishing the season on 20 goals in all competitions, closely followed by Ian Taylor with 16. Taylor's fine performances earned him a £1m move to Sheffield Wednesday in the summer of 1994 as Vale looked forward to their return to the second tier. John Rudge and chairman Bill Bell were able to use the transfer windfall from the Taylor sale to bring in three players who would come to define the Valiants through the rest of the decade and make their marks on the Potteries derbies to come – Tony Naylor, Steve Guppy and Ian Bogie. Vale then made a relatively steady start to life in the First Division, very much a win one-lose one opening salvo, before a tough winter run saw them slide down towards a relegation scrap.

Stoke had made a solid mid-table return to the second tier in 1993/94, despite losing star striker Stein to a £1.4 million move to Chelsea. The 'Golden One' had already racked up 13 goals by October, including cup heroics against Manchester United, so it was no surprise that the bigger teams came sniffing for the prolific goalscorer. Stein actually finished the season as Stoke's second-highest goalscorer despite only playing 12 league games.

Surprisingly, Stein's departure wasn't even the most significant move away from the Vic for the Potters at that time. In October 1993 the hugely popular manager Lou Macari left to join his boyhood club Celtic. The move was a bitter disappointment for Stoke fans, and the hope was that his replacement would be someone of equal or greater popularity, such as club legend and Meir lad Denis Smith. Instead, chairman Peter Coates opted for another Scot, bringing in the no-nonsense Joe Jordan, who was coincidentally joining after a spell on the coaching staff at Celtic. Jordan already had a job on his hands to win over the Potters' fans – he wasn't Lou Macari, he wasn't Denis Smith, and his football wasn't the prettiest to behold. After a mixed start to the 1994/95 season, two consecutive 4-0 losses spelled the end for the unpopular Jordan. Yet another Scot,

Asa Hartford, took temporary charge after Jordan's departure, before Macari made his triumphant return to the Potteries following an unsuccessful spell in Glasgow. With the various player and managerial shuffling out of the way, we were back to Macari v Rudge in the Potteries.

* * *

The way that the fixture list had churned out meant that the two Potteries sides wouldn't actually meet for the first league tie until 14 March 1995. Both teams were sitting uncomfortably above the relegation zone, with a slight cushion but still a feeling of unease about their risky positions. Once again the Vale Park pitch was heavy, but it still only took the home side three minutes to break the deadlock with new boy Tony Naylor marking his Potteries derby debut with a lashing finish after a flowing Vale move. The other derby debutant, Steve Guppy, was causing constant problems too, as Stoke floundered and flopped like, well, a guppy.

Despite taking an early battering and being caught shell-shocked, Stoke began trawling for an equaliser and with Gleghorn hooking in a free kick, Lee Sandford used his mussel to win his header, which found the Vale net (OK, enough of these cod-awful fish puns). Lee Glover, Robin van der Laan and Alan

Tankard would go close for the Vale, and Stoke's own derby debutant Toddy Örlygsson threatened for the visitors, but the game ended 1-1, a point which didn't really settle the nerves of either set of fans. The attendance of 19,510 was once again the highest home gate of the season.

Due to the rather bizarre fixture arrangements, the return game at the Vic came just over a month later. The crowd of 20,429 was again the highest of the campaign as the two teams met in what were slightly less precarious circumstances. Though not yet guaranteed, both rivals were more or less safe with four games to go; Stoke had found their form under Macari from the end of March to record just one loss in their last seven outings, while a win at home to Burnley had helped Vale creep away from the trapdoor. The game was still important to both sets of fans, both for local bragging rights and to determine which team would finish higher up the league. The game got under way with a flurry of red, white, yellow and black balloons blowing across the pitch. It was another typically wet and windy Stoke-on-Trent day, but the match lacked the blood and thunder of some of the previous meetings. Stoke's Canadian striker Paul Peschisolido looked the most likely to make something happen for the home side, going close a couple of times in the first half. Despite

Stoke's pressure, chances were few and far between and it remained 0-0 at half-time.

As had been the case in previous meetings at the Vic, Vale came out much stronger after the break, with Naylor forcing Ronnie Sinclair into an early save after the striker was given a chance to go through, but Naylor wasn't able to bear down enough on the City goal to take full advantage of the opportunity. Vale were looking to catch Stoke on the break but it was the Potters who nearly took the lead after a long free kick forward was cushioned on by John Gayle, but Gleghorn's header went wide of the post, their best chance of the game. It would prove costly as a minute later, more trickery from Guppy down the left wing won Vale a corner. Guppy took the set piece himself, sending in an inviting cross for the prolific Martin Foyle to head home in front of the joyous away end. 'We hate Stoke!', 'One-nil to the Port Vale!' and 'Rudgie's Barmy Army!' were now ringing around the famous old ground.

Vale continued to look threatening, building play down both wings and peppering the Stoke box with crosses. Peschisolido was still looking dangerous for Stoke, forcing Musselwhite to save remarkably down to his left, tipping the Canadian's shot on to the post, before the loose ball was scrambled away. Stoke's hopes of finding an equaliser were dealt a big blow when Ian Cranson went in hard on a 50/50 and was second to the ball, resulting in a second yellow card with a little under ten minutes remaining. It was seen as a harsh decision at the time but nowadays, it'd probably be a straight red, especially if VAR was involved. From that point on, Vale were able to see out the game. John Rudge had masterminded another Port Vale win at the Victoria Ground, exorcising the same demon that he had partially vanquished with the Autoglass Trophy victory, but this time it was in the league – their first such result at the Vic since 1927.

Both teams found themselves mathematically safe by the end of the day and Stoke would go on to end the season with seven points from nine, catapulting themselves up to 11th. Vale finished in 17th but with a draw and a win in the two league meetings, they would have felt very happy with their Potteries derby showings for the season, taking the bragging rights and wallowing in their victory on the turf of their most bitter enemy. It certainly wasn't the most spectacular of seasons for the two clubs, at least compared to the exploits of 1992/93, but Foyle's winner was another memorable moment for the travelling Vale fans in ST4. Having spent so much of their recent history in different divisions, it was a nice change to know that the two clubs would meet again in the 1995/96 season. Not since the 1950s had they played each other in consecutive league seasons.

* * *

1995 was a pivotal year for Stoke City, as newly appointed chief executive Jez Moxey started to make his mark on the club. Planned development of the Victoria Ground in May, which was to include the development of a new 9,000 all-seater stand at a cost of £5m, was scrapped. Instead, Moxey pushed successfully for a different plan to move the club to a new purpose-built stadium. The Potters had played at the Vic since 1878 and was the club's spiritual home in the middle of the town of Stoke-upon-Trent, but the combination of the release of the Taylor Report, the likely costs of a full refurbishment and Moxey's desire to stamp Stoke as a potential Premier League team meant the move would be inevitable.

There were still at least a couple of seasons at the Victoria Ground to be played out though, and with Macari now fully re-settled, the overall feeling around the club was positive and looking forwards. Striker Mike Sheron would be the most notable new signing of 1995/96, arriving in a swap deal for the fruitless Keith Scott, though the general make-up of the team was to remain relatively unchanged from the previous few campaigns. Over in Burslem, John

Rudge brought in Lee Mills, with Robin van der Laan moving in the opposite direction to Derby County, and Jon McCarthy also arrived as a club record signing for £500,000 from York City. The Valiants started the season poorly, picking up just one point from the opening two games and failing to find the net in either of them. Stoke picked up four points from their first two. In the previous season, the two Potteries teams had to wait seven months for their first meeting of the season. In 1995/96, they only had to wait until the third match.

Prior to kick-off, there was something of a treat for those early to their seats or standing positions. Potteries hero Sir Stanley Matthews was on hand to wave to the supporters, but he wasn't the only familiar local face to grace the crowd with his presence. Fresh from his controversial departure from Britain's biggest boy band, Take That, Tunstall lad and Port Vale fan Robbie Williams emerged from the Family Paddock to a sea of jeers from the Stoke City fans, and chants of 'You're not singing anymore!' *The Sentinel*'s Pete Smith commented on Robbie's Vic appearance, 'I'm not sure why anyone would have expected a different reception. Stoke fans rip into supporters getting engaged and tear into marching bands, so a celebrity Vale fan from a boy band was not going to be politely clapped like he'd come out to open the batting at Lord's!'

Williams wasn't exactly a household name in August 1995, but there was certainly a particular demographic who were aware of him. Another more mature demographic was probably more familiar with his father, Pete Conway, who was a local performer around the Stoke-on-Trent clubs and pubs. The game was covered live by Central TV, which must have had a notable effect on the matchday attendance. The final crowd number was a very modest 14,283, less than half the average for the 17 derbies staged at Stoke since 1920 and the first to fall below 20,000. Both the home and away sections had notable gaps, though those in attendance still made it a fiery pre-match atmosphere.

Stoke were particularly sluggish in the first half, despite the hot atmosphere, as the visitors assumed control through some tidy midfield play. Overson and Gleghorn went close for the home side, but the rather tepid first half ended 0-0 with neither goalkeeper really troubled. Vale would have been the happier of the two sides and had shown themselves to be a bit of a second-half team throughout the season, so it wasn't a complete surprise when the visitors took the lead just three minutes after the restart. Lee Glover slid the ball through towards Ian Bogie on the right side of the Stoke penalty area. Bogie managed to fend off the challenge of Overson with a turn of pace, before somehow squeezing it under the keeper from

an acute angle to give Vale the lead. Stoke keeper
Carl Muggleton would have felt disappointed to have
been beaten at his near post. After that, Stoke never
really got going. Peschisolido worked Musselwhite in
search of an equaliser, and substitute Simon Sturridge
spurned the best chance for the home team, lobbing
wide of the post with only the goalkeeper to beat and
time running out. Once again, though, Port Vale ran
out 1-0 winners at the Victoria Ground. Like First
PMT buses, Vale waited an age for one to come along
and then two arrived in quick succession.

Straight after the final whistle, Port Vale manager
John Rudge beamed as he commented, 'It's a great
result. It wasn't a vintage performance or vintage game,
but we've managed to win a Potteries derby, and that's
important to us. It was good build-up play for the goal,
and Ian managed to squeeze it in at the near post.
We've managed to get the three points, and obviously
our supporters will be delighted with the result.' He
was right, of course, and by contrast, the Stoke fans
had given their own players the same treatment that
Robbie Williams had received a couple of hours earlier.
There were cries of 'What a load of rubbish' from the
home stands, after what could only be described as
one of the more passionless and sluggish local derbies
in living memory. *The Sentinel* described Stoke's play
as 'too ponderous and slow', while *The Independent*

wrote that Sturridge's late miss was 'an indication of Stoke's lethargy and lack of imagination', before adding that the attendance below 20,000 was 'unlikely to be the last'.

You wouldn't find too many Vale fans grumbling about the quality of the game or lack of vitality, as lightning had now struck twice at Stoke's spiritual home, with in all likelihood one more Potteries derby to be played there before the move to the new stadium. The loss was the start of a poor run of form for the Potters, who lost their next three and only managed three wins in their opening 14 games. They were looking toothless and lethargic, but the impending signing of Sheron would change all that in the winter months. For the Vale, their form took a similar trajectory, having to wait seven more games before their second victory of the season, before going a further eight without a win up to December. Eventually, with new signings settling in, both teams would pick up before the new year.

* * *

The return meeting was on 12 March 1996, a night match in Burslem under the lights. Though their form had picked up since Christmas, Vale found themselves second from bottom in the table. They had, however, won their last outing at home to Southend United, part of a six-game unbeaten run that included four straight draws. A fine November run which saw Stoke win six of their seven fixtures, followed up by a run of six unbeaten leading up to the Potteries derby, meant they were now sitting in the play-off positions. New signing Sheron was establishing himself as a regular goalscorer, forming a strong SAS partnership with Simon Sturridge up top.

This time, it wasn't windy and rainy in Staffordshire. No, it was snowing instead. Port Vale had earlier made an appeal to fans to go down to the ground to help clear the pitch of snow in order for the match to go ahead. The call was answered, and the pitch was lined with walls of piled-up snow. The game got under way at a snowy Vale Park and, well, why don't I just give you the BBC Radio Stoke opening match coverage from commentator George Andrews:

'The game has just got under way, and to take us through the teams, here's ... but on the attack straight away is Ian Bogie. GOOOOOAL, IAN BOGIE, BOGIE'S DONE THE BUSINESS! FIVE SECONDS INTO THE GAME, THE BOGIE BOOGIE HAS SET IT ALIGHT HERE, AND THE STOKIES ARE STUNNED. PORT VALE ONE, STOKE CITY NIL!'

Yes, another iconic Potteries derby moment under the lights at Vale Park. Most fans had barely taken their seats, and no doubt many probably missed the goal or weren't paying full attention, but everyone could now witness the sight of the Vale players dancing around in the snow, kicking it and throwing it around like kids in a Christmas card.

It was actually 12 seconds, not five. Still Port Vale's fastest ever goal, though it's 71st in the all-time rankings of fastest goals in association football, four places ahead of goalkeeper Asmir Begović's 2013 goal for Stoke against Southampton. As for the goal itself, it came straight from the kick-off with skipper Andy Porter playing the ball to defender Andy Hill. His forward pass was left by Martin Foyle for Bogie to catch out the sleeping Stoke defence, and carry the ball towards the right side of the penalty box before hammering it into the top-left corner, smashing into the stanchion and nestling in Mark Prudhoe's goal. As Valiants supporter Barry Seaton described it, 'A quite beautiful, crisp late-season evening, snow clearers (i.e., fans), banter with Eric Bristow, draught Bass and pies at the Park Inn, what could be better? Well, this could … Andy Hill, Vale full-back, pushes a trademark pass through the inside-right channel to Lee Glover, whose skills included this dummy out of the way and to the left. The pass travelled on to Foyle, who feinted a touch. Through a gap diagonally and behind the ball was Ian Bogie, barrelling at pace with short legs and high skill. At the edge of the box, the pass had barely been touched. Bogie caught the ball up, pushed it on to volley at an angle from the edge over Prudhoe for what would now be called a Worldie. The game was 12 seconds old.'

Vale assumed control after that, knocking the ball around nicely on the peppered white pitch. Lee Glover twice stung the palms of Prudhoe before Stoke finally found their way into the game. Kevin Keen brought the ball down the left, playing in Sturridge with his back to goal. Sturridge laid it off to Sheron, who powered a shot to Musselwhite's right, but the ball smashed off the inside of the post and somehow went out for a goal kick on the opposite side. In the second half, Stoke went in search of an equaliser, and their first goal against the Vale in over two and a half games. Sheron, Sturridge and Gleghorn went close but it was all to no avail. That Bogie moment is pretty much ingrained in the minds of those in attendance that day. While it is probably a personal highlight for most Vale supporters, Kirsty, co-host of the *Ale and the Vale* podcast, doesn't look back on it so fondly, 'One of my worst moments was probably bad for different reasons to other fans. Hearing Bogie score on the radio, but not being there because my mum wouldn't let me go because of the possible trouble. I just wanted to be there celebrating.'

Another Potteries derby win for Port Vale, and another 1-0 scoreline. It was now three 1-0 victories in a row, two thanks to Ian Bogie, and the Valiants' first league double over the Potters since 1925. Another long-standing record broken by Rudge's men.

* * *

After the game, Bogie would describe his two derby goals as 'extra special' in his thick Geordie accent, adding, 'It's a great occasion to play in these Potteries derbies, a great atmosphere.' He would later recall the moment, describing the 12-second strike as one of his best. He said, 'The games against Stoke City were always big and the two league games in the 1995/96 season were big highlights of my career. The game where I scored after 12 seconds was a great game to win as it came before our [Anglo-Italian] cup final against Genoa. I can't remember too much about the game, but I do know that goal is on YouTube to this day, and it must count as one of my best ever goals.'

The win moved Vale out of the bottom three, and as Bogie had remembered, they were about to challenge for the Anglo-Italian Cup. The now-defunct competition ran intermittently between 1970 and 1996 between clubs from England and Italy and had become a bit of a focal point for violence between opposition supporters, meaning at times matches were abandoned, tournaments were cancelled, and the format was changed. 1996 would be the last year of the competition, so Vale were the last English club to progress all the way to the final. Stoke had taken part in the competition in 1971 and 1972, and again from 1993 to 1996, reaching the semi-final in 1995. This was Vale's one and only participation in the tournament, meeting Genoa in the final on 17 March at a sparsely attended Wembley Stadium. Foyle netted twice for the Vale but Genoa ran out 5-2 winners, with former Italian international Gennaro Ruotolo scoring a hat-trick in a game which also featured Vincenzo Montella and John van 't Schip. It had been a good run for the Valiants, overcoming teams such as Cesena, Ancona and Perugia, as well as beating off domestic competition from Birmingham, Oldham, Luton, Ipswich and West Brom.

The Potteries derby victory was part of a remarkable run of six straight wins for Vale as they climbed up towards mid-table. For Stoke, it was one defeat of three in a blip that saw Macari's men go five without victory. However, they would regain their winning habit at the start of April and finish the season strongly, with Sheron hitting a white-hot goalscoring streak, scoring in seven consecutive games.

A final-day home win against Southend meant that the Potters finished fourth and would face Martin O'Neill's Leicester City in the play-offs. Leicester were a strong team, but Stoke had already done the league double over them so confidence was high, especially with Sheron and Sturridge up front. Stoke dominated the first leg at Filbert Street but would rue missed chances. Graham Potter spurned the best opportunity to open the scoring, and it would prove costly as Leicester won the second leg 1-0 thanks to Garry Parker, and the Foxes would go on to seal promotion to the Premier League. The two games lost in the two Potteries derby were the difference makers in the end for Stoke, who had finished six points behind second-placed Derby County. The Rams were promoted due in no small part to the goals and captaincy of former Vale star Robin van der Laan.

* * *

While Stoke had the better season overall, finishing fourth and unlucky to fall short in the play-offs, 1995/96 was another notch in the belt for Port Vale. A mid-table finish coupled with their first Potteries derby double in 70 years, Rudge was cementing his legacy as the Valiants' greatest ever manager. It was now four derby games without defeat going back to early 1993. The following season, Vale would be well positioned to give promotion a genuine attempt while also looking to score one final win over Stoke at the Victoria Ground.

For Stoke fans, many were still coming to terms with the upcoming move to Trentham Lakes. Lou Macari would be hoping for another push for promotion, but with the mounting costs of the stadium move he wasn't likely to receive much financial backing from Peter Coates and Keith Humphreys for the endeavour. In fact, crowd favourites Nigel Gleghorn, Vince Overson and Graham Potter all departed as the reality of the move set in on supporters. Times were a-changin' at Stoke.

There weren't any notable changes at Vale Park, as Rudge continued to keep faith with the core squad that had brought steady progress throughout the 1990s. The front three of Martin Foyle, Lee Mills and Tony Naylor were tasked with maintaining fitness and regular goals for the season ahead, backed up by the likes of Steve Guppy, Andy Porter, Stewart Talbot and Ian Bogie. Lee Glover departed for Rotherham, while rumours began to circulate about the highly rated Guppy and his chances of lasting the season with Vale. Chairman Bill Bell was gaining a reputation for turning Vale into a selling club, with star players such as Ian Taylor and Robin van der Laan already moving on to bigger and better things while the Valiants had remained static.

Vale made a slow start, winless in their first three, though a satisfying 6-1 aggregate League Cup win over

Crewe Alexandra gave the fans something to cheer about. Their poor start would continue throughout September, leading up to the first Potteries derby of the season at Vale Park on 13 October 1996. Stoke had made a surprisingly good start, finding themselves as season table-toppers, with Lou Macari winning the manager of the month award for August. Mike Sheron had picked up where he left off the previous season, netting six times in the opening five league games. Back-to-back defeats to Barnsley and Birmingham brought everyone back down to earth though, while a last-minute equaliser from new signing Graham Kavanagh rescued a point for the Potters at Bolton prior to the derby. The financial elephant in the room was limited funds raised to date for outgoing players and a £6m stadium bill imminent. Some of the pressure was alleviated with the announcement of a new shirt and ground sponsorship deal with Leek-based Britannia Building Society, and thus the new ground would be christened the Britannia Stadium.

The first Potteries derby of the 1996/97 season was held on a surprisingly sunny Sunday afternoon in Burslem. The pitch was in fine condition; another sign of the changing times. It was, however, a windy day, which would have an adverse effect on the match quality. The attendance of 14,396 was another reflection of the feeling of apathy and disgruntlement among the Vale support with their board, meaning there was more or less a 50/50 split between the Stoke fans packed in behind the goal in the Hamil Road End, and the Vale fans occupying the three home stands. The chants of 'sh*t ground, no fans' and 'you couldn't sell all your tickets', plus home chants of 'sack the board', were pretty reflective of the curiously low turnout.

The game started quickly, with Gerry McMahon testing Vale's Dutch goalkeeper Arjan van Heusden early on before Guppy almost sneaked through to catch out the Stoke defence at the other end. But things soon settled down and the wind started to prevent any solid build-up play in the first half. Any fluid football for the visitors was coming from the on-loan Kavanagh, who was already looking like a shrewd bit of business for Macari. Fellow new signing Gerry McMahon went closest for the visitors before half-time, striking a powerful effort at goal from the right-hand side of the box which was tipped over by van Heusden. The first half ended goalless.

A strong first-half challenge from Andy Porter on McMahon meant that the Northern Irishman didn't emerge for the second half, replaced at half-time by Kevin Keen. Not a minute after the resumption, Ian Bogie went down in a heap just in front of the dugouts after a challenge from Richard Forsyth. John

Rudge accompanied the paramedics on to the pitch to check on the condition of the midfielder as the home fans jeered the lack of action from the referee. The Stoke supporters cheered as the match-winner of the previous two derbies was stretchered off, replaced by Lee Mills.

The game opened up in the second half, with Sheron looking ever dangerous, and Ray Wallace going close. After sustained pressure from the Potters, a high ball forward from Ally Pickering was met by the substitute Keen, whose looping header bent in the air like a penny floater, creeping in at the far post to give Stoke the lead. Fireworks went off in the away end as the Stoke fans celebrated their first goal against Vale since March 1995. Stoke withstood an aerial bombardment after that, and with the clock ticking down, some Vale supporters began to head for an early exit. But those who remained were rewarded for their loyalty, as in the third minute of injury time Steve Guppy pumped one final hopeful ball forward, and with goalkeeper Prudhoe challenging, substitute Mills rose highest to head the ball in for the equaliser. The fans who had remained poured on to the pitch to celebrate, and then poured back into the stands to taunt the dejected Stokies with the old classic 'You're not singing anymore!' and the newly minted 'You'll never beat the Vale!'

After the game, Rudge said, 'It was a scrappy game, typical of a derby with not a lot of football being played and not a lot of quality on the pitch from both sides. It was a case of scrapping it out. I felt that their goal was from a ball high up in the air and it was a nothing goal really, poor from our sense. I don't think either side created many chances. With Bogie coming off with a bad injury, we put Millsy on hoping we would get a little bit of joy from his height in the air, and he produced that in the dying seconds. Our supporters will go home the happier I think.' Macari commented, 'We gave them a chance in the 90th minute, an easy ball into the box. We were praying for a ball in for our goalkeeper to come out and catch for game over, but unfortunately, through a jump with Mills, the ball ended up in the back of the net. Very disappointed. We've thrown away two points.'

I guess you could say there were positives to take for Stoke fans. Many would have taken a draw at Vale Park, particularly given the recent Potteries derby results. They managed to end the run of 1-0 defeats and even managed to score a long-overdue goal too. Macari declared that the performance was 'a lot better than we've done here in the past'. But once again, it would be the Vale fans who could carry themselves with a bit of a swagger at work and school on Monday morning, pinching the late equaliser to anger and frustrate their Stoke City counterparts. It was now five derbies without a win for Stoke, and only two wins from ten since the sides had been reacquainted in 1989. They were without a victory at home against the Valiants since October 1992, with only one Potteries derby left to play at the Victoria Ground.

* * *

The two teams wouldn't meet for the second derby until 20 April 1997, the penultimate league game and final derby at the Victoria Ground. From 1887 to the last meeting, the Vic had hosted 24 league and domestic cup clashes between the two sides, plus dozens of friendlies, minor cup and regional league fixtures. The total number of games at Stoke's long-standing home was 88, with the Potters winning 54 of them. But it was Vale who had been feeling at home in Stoke town centre in recent years, winning on their last three visits down Boothen Old Road and undefeated there in four. By their final Vic meeting, Stoke were stranded in mid-table, having been unable to mount a consistent run of form since the turn of the year, while Vale were riding high in sixth position, surfing a wave of momentum after four straight wins had put them in play-off contention. 'Rudge was on the verge of the greatest miracle since Lazarus. Little Bozlem mixing it with Arsenal, Manchester United and Newcastle,' as described by Barry Seaton.

Just 24 hours before the historic clash, Stoke fans were once again rocked by yet another significant club announcement. The hugely popular manager Lou Macari announced that he was quitting his role at the end of the season, to pursue his claim for unfair dismissal against Celtic. Macari stated that he needed to concentrate on 'a match I need to win more than any I've been involved in', adding that he would be ruined if the verdict went against him, with legal costs estimated at around £450,000. 'If I lose this case, I'll be selling *The Big Issue* the next day,' he said.

The news came as a big issue to the Stoke board, who now needed to find a new manager to take the club forward to the Britannia Stadium. Macari's parting with the club would be less amicable than he would have hoped, with Peter Coates reportedly stripping the manager of his duties before he could leave on his own terms, resulting in yet more lawsuits for unfair dismissal. That was all still to come though.

The televised derby would be my first personal derby in attendance, and there was a real carnival feel around the ground pre-kick-off – balloons, bucket hats, face paint, cheerleaders, sunshine, the lot. The Stoke fans were given at least some good news in the build-up with 22-goal man Mike Sheron declared fit after a recent injury. Vale were without Steve Guppy, who had moved to Leicester City for £850,000 earlier in the season, but that hadn't halted their progress. Stoke were turning up to win their last home derby game at the Vic and halt Vale's promotion push; Vale were there to spoil the party and inflict one last defeat on Macari at the old ground, on their march up the league.

* * *

The Vale fans were in full p*sstake mode before kick-off, waving their arms to the tune of 'Bye bye Lou Macari'. In a closely contested opening 45 minutes, Carl Beeston and Richard Forsyth tested Musselwhite with a couple of tame efforts. Jon McCarthy would also keep the tracksuit bottoms-clad Muggleton busy with several crosses from the right. On 35 minutes, the game burst into life as a late Koordes challenge on Pickering led to a skirmish between the two sides. A couple of minutes later, Wallace and Porter had a smaller altercation as tempers became frayed.

With a minute to go to half-time, the ball came to Sheron midway inside the Vale half. The striker dinked past three challenges before rifling a right-footed shot which rattled off Dean Glover's chest and settled in the bottom corner of the net. Seconds later, the half-time whistle blew as the Stoke fans were still celebrating their lead.

The Victoria Ground in the heart of Stoke town centre, Stoke City's home from 1878 until 1997

Vale Park has been Port Vale's home ground in Burslem since 1950

Hanley-born Stanley Matthews, who played for Stoke City and managed Port Vale

Port Vale's legendary manager John Rudge, in his familiar attire

Stoke manager Lou Macari looks on from the dugout (and my mum in the paddock in the foreground!)

Port Vale goalkeeper Paul Musselwhite played in numerous Potteries derby matches

Two local lads who made their marks on the world in their own ways. Tunstall-born multi-platinum album selling pop star and Port Vale fan Robbie Williams (left), and the 'Wizard of Dribble' Sir Stanley Matthews. Picture (courtesy of Pete Smith and The Sentinel)

The last Potteries derby at the Victoria Ground breaks down

The Vale Park pitch receiving a watering. Sometimes Mother Nature would provide a little too much water...

A move to Trentham Lakes was on the horizon for the Potters in 1997

A familiar obstructing view in front of the away end for a Potteries derby

Port Vale striker Tony Naylor gets away from Stoke defender Ally Pickering during a Potteries derby

Stoke's former manager Guðjón Thórdarson (left), with director of football John Rudge

Lee Mills, who represented both clubs, in Potteries derby action

Dave Brammer played for Stoke City, Port Vale and Crewe Alexandra

Five of the six towns of Stoke-on-Trent (Fenton omitted, much like in Arnold Bennett's work)

Stoke 1
← Burslem 5
Tunstall 6

Longton 1¼ →
Hanley 1¾

The Valiants were hunting for an equaliser in the second half, making for a greater spectacle as the game opened up. Lou's own son Mike Macari went close to doubling Stoke's lead, hitting the crossbar from an overhead kick. McCarthy threatened for Vale, forcing a low block from a combination of Muggleton and Pickering on the line. With just over five minutes remaining a Glover clearance was charged down on the edge of the penalty area, ricocheting into the path of the predator Sheron, who struck it past Musselwhite with venom. For the first time in a long time, Stoke fans could relax in a Potteries derby, knowing victory was all but assured. The final Potteries derby at the Victoria Ground ended Stoke City 2 Port Vale 0.

For some Vale fans, it was all too much to witness a rare defeat at the hands of their neighbours; Tom from the *Ale and the Vale* podcast recounts, 'I've been relatively lucky in my lifetime to have only ever seen us lose once to Stoke. It was the 2-0 defeat at the Victoria Ground, Sheron megging Musselwhite to make it two … and I cried!'

For Lou Macari, it was the end of 'a rollercoaster 48 hours', commenting that the occasion was Stoke's 'last shot at doing something for our fans'. There was still time for one last win over another rival, West Bromwich Albion, in the last league game of the season, but it was the end of two eras at Stoke

– Macari, and the Victoria Ground. For Rudge, the result meant that his team would need to produce two positive results against Wolves and Crystal Palace to sustain their promotion challenge, which they were not able to do. The Valiants wouldn't be visiting the likes of Old Trafford and Anfield for league games in 1997/98, but they would be visiting the Britannia Stadium.

8

Crossing the Divide

A QUICK digression before moving on to 1997/98 (any excuse as a Stoke fan to avoid discussing that season).

As many as 100 players have turned out for both Potteries clubs, plus countless others who will have been on the books at some youth level before ending up on the other side of the city. As already mentioned earlier in this book, Robbie Earle is one example of such a transfer. Of the 100 known moves, half of them were directly from one club to the other. Pre-1930, swapping back and forth between local clubs was commonplace, as big-money transfers and travelling around distant cities weren't really the norm. One of the more notable early movers was Congleton-born England international right-back Tommy Clare, who started out at Burslem Port Vale then moved to Stoke in 1884, making over 250 appearances for the Potters before spending two more spells at Vale. Billy Heames moved to Vale in 1897, making 233 appearances and scoring 26 goals. Tom Holford, who made a record 28 appearances in derby games, played 269 games for Stoke and 56 for Vale. Wilf Kirkham, Port Vale's all-time record goalscorer, would play 276 games for them from 1923 to 1933, with a few years at Stoke sandwiched in between 1929 and 1932. Kirkham scored 164 goals for Vale, including a club record 41 in the 1926/27 campaign and seven against Stoke, and netted 30 times for the Potters too. Arthur Bridgett, considered more of a hero in the red of white of Sunderland than Stoke, also represented both clubs, making a remarkable and triumphant return to league football for Vale in 1923, 11 years after his previous appearance for the Mackems and into his 40s.

As discussed earlier on, Freddie Steele would make himself a legend at both Stoke and Vale between 1933 and 1953, scoring 140 goals for the Potters and 12 for the Valiants, as well as successfully managing Vale in two separate spells between 1951 and 1965. We also saw how Sir Stanley Matthews faired in his short management stint at Vale Park, though his playing legacy had already earned him respect from supporters of both clubs. By the 1970s and '80s, a few more household names would turn out for both sides. Stoke's record appearance maker Eric Skeels played a handful of times for Vale, as did League Cup winners Alan Bloor and Jimmy Greenhoff. Bill Bentley, who made 48 appearances for Stoke between 1964 and 1968, went on to play 95 times for Vale in the late '70s, even briefly managing them in 1979. At the time of writing Bill can still be found working as a window cleaner around the local area. Stoke-on-Trent-born brothers Mark and Neville Chamberlain both started their careers at Port Vale before moving to the Victoria Ground in 1982. Mark's Stoke career would be by far the more notable of the two. When asked if the move led to any stick thrown his way from mates, he said, 'No, not really. Mind you it wouldn't, I didn't really have any mates!'

Post-1990s moves have included modern Vale legends such as Lee Mills and Steve Guppy turning out sporadically for Tony Pulis's Stoke. Mills managed a couple of goals in his 11 appearances for the side that fought off relegation in 2003, scoring a cracker to equalise late on against Norwich City and hitting the winner at home to Walsall in the second half of the season, important contributions as Stoke survived by four points. Guppy would only make four appearances for Stoke in 2004. Neil MacKenzie, part of the Potters' doomed 1998 squad, would eventually make a few appearances at Vale Park, and two players on loan at Stoke during their 2002 promotion campaign, Ian Brightwell and Tony Dinning, would also go on to make 41 and 48 appearances for Vale respectively in the early to mid-2000s. Gareth Owen started out at Stoke, later becoming a player-coach at Vale Park, and Tunstall's own Martin Paterson would also represent both sides. Michael Tonge, who only made 12 appearances for Stoke but somehow stuck around for five years at the Britannia Stadium, moved to Vale in 2017. Former Stoke favourites Ronnie Sinclair and Dean Whitehead are both on the current coaching staff at Vale Park. Stoke cult legend Carl Dickinson, who was the poster boy of their promotion to the Premier League in 2008 thanks to his passion and rapport with supporters, joined Vale in 2013, becoming a favourite on the other side of the city too. Dickinson was recently the player-manager of Hanley Town, playing alongside another ex-Stoke and Vale player, Danny Pugh. In July 2022, Alsager-born Will Forrester, who came through the youth ranks at Stoke, made the rare direct permanent switch to Port Vale – and caused a bit of a stir online. Stoke youngster Liam McCarron also joined the Valiants on loan for the 2022/23 season, suggesting a closer working relationship between the two clubs than has existed in recent memory.

Angela Smith reflected on some of the cross-city switches, 'When you look back at the games and some of the characters involved from both teams, you realise how football has changed. The local rivalry meant so much more than it seems to nowadays. I often wonder how players that crossed the divide felt. To this day I still call Terry Lees a traitor when I see him, but I forgive Jimmy Greenhoff! You look at the list of players that went from Stoke to Vale or vice versa and Mark Chamberlain in the most recent times is the only player who improved his career prospects by crossing the divide.'

* * *

Perhaps the most high-profile player to play for both clubs in modern times, notable by his absence in the list so far, is midfielder Dave Brammer. Brammer was a regular at Port Vale between 1999 and 2001, making his own mark on the Potteries derby (coming up). He was one of an exclusive list to play for Port Vale, Stoke City and Crewe Alexandra, moving to the Alexandra Stadium from Vale in 2001 having been named their player of the year in 2000. Alex boss Dario Gradi described the £500,000 signing of Brammer as 'probably the biggest in our history', adding, 'For us to be signing Dave Brammer from Port Vale is such a major step.'

Valiant 2001, the fan-based group that was formed to take over Port Vale after years of frustration with the board, issued a statement condemning the decision to sell Brammer:

'We finished last season on a high with a long unbeaten run and success in the LDV [Vans Trophy] final at Cardiff. Within the space of three short months, we've lost last season's top scorer, our most creative midfield player and now, it would appear, our player of the year. Not to mention two other very experienced squad professionals. The loss of these five key players is a massive blow. But even more damaging perhaps is the adverse effect on the morale of management, other playing staff and supporters. What a way to start the season.

'As far as Valiant 2001 is concerned, the release and sale of these players has nothing to do with the interests of Port Vale Football Club and everything to do with alleviating the financial pressure which the board, by a succession of poor decisions, has allowed to build up to almost unbearable proportions. Unfortunately, it's typical of the knee-jerk short-termism we've come to expect from the Vale. There has to be a better way than this. Maybe if the members of the board spent more time putting in place a proper business strategy, and less getting themselves embroiled in all manner of costly legal wrangles, the club wouldn't have to sell its best player to the first bidder waving a cheque book. The chairman [Bill Bell] may well have bought himself a little time. But, Valiant 2001 would ask, at what cost to the long-term future of Port Vale Football Club?'

Brammer made 87 appearances for the Railwaymen between 2001 and 2004, before joining Tony Pulis's Potters at the end of his contract. He was one of Pulis's trusted midfield generals, a player who knew how to follow instructions and patiently play in the manager's infamous cage system. Brammer only managed three goals for Stoke, though they were all pretty spectacular. He eventually returned to Vale Park under manager Dean Glover in 2008 for a few loan appearances, before joining permanently from Millwall in the summer of the same year. After being informed by Vale chairman and former key figure of Valiant 2001 Bill Bratt that he wouldn't be offered a new contract, notified by voicemail message, Brammer stated, 'I checked my phone, and the message was left saying I wouldn't be getting anything. Having been at the club twice now, I thought he could have phoned me back and spoken to me.'

* * *

A handful of staff members have also crossed the divide to represent both clubs as a player and in a coaching or directing capacity. Hanley-born Joe Schofield played 199 times for Stoke between 1891 and 1899 before managing the Potters between 1915 and 1919. He was replaced as manager by Arthur Shallcross, and opted to join Port Vale in 1920. Former

Stoke loanee Micky Adams managed Vale across two different spells between 2009 and 2014, following in the path of other former Potters players to take the Vale Park job, such as Bill Bentley, Alan Bloor and Stanley Matthews.

Dave Brammer may have been the most high-profile player move of modern times, but that pales in comparison to one that caught everyone in the city off-guard – John Rudge. Yes, the flat-capped one was doing the unthinkable, joining the club that he had so very often gone into battle with from the other side of the divide. Rudge's tenure at Vale Park ended in January 1999, with the club once again fighting relegation. His sacking by chairman Bill Bell was met with a flat-cap protest from more than 400 fans. It was understandable; Rudge was one of a kind in English football management. Fans even released 843 black and white balloons, representing the number of games Rudge took charge of for the Valiants.

In some ways, Rudge is Vale's own version of a Sir Stanley Matthews. He isn't originally from the city, but he epitomises the club and is part of the very fabric, loved by fans and always represented on the pitch by his well-assembled teams. His ability to pick a player from unknown parts of both the UK and Europe and then negotiate a deal were unmatched. His list of signings who would go on to reach greater heights (and be sold for a profit) includes Mark Bright, Robbie Earle, Robin van der Laan, Gareth Ainsworth, Ian Taylor, Steve Guppy, Jon McCarthy, Lee Mills, Marcus Bent and Anthony Gardner. Following Rudge's dismissal, even the great Sir Alex Ferguson said, 'Every Port Vale supporter should get down on their knees and thank the lord for John Rudge.'

Commenting on his fondest memories with BBC Radio Stoke, Rudge recalled, 'Our three Wembley visits: the play-offs against West Brom, the Anglo-Italian Cup against Genoa, and also the LDV Vans Trophy victory. Although we lost against Genoa and the Baggies, they are still great days in the club's history, and we certainly made up for it in our win against Stockport. Over 19 years we had some fantastic FA Cup runs. We beat Everton and Tottenham. Getting Port Vale into the Second Division for the first time in 33 years was also a great achievement.'

Discussing his departure, Rudge said, 'Nineteen years was a long time. I was sacked and asked to be director of football, but I thought it was the right time for me to leave, because I didn't think my relationship then with the board of directors was as good as I would have liked it to have been. It was always an awkward situation and I think the main reason I stayed as long as I did was down to the supporters, because they were fantastic to me.'

After turning down the director of football role at Vale Park, Rudge accepted the same position at the Britannia Stadium. Though it was a bitter pill for Vale fans to swallow, they could at least find solace in the fact that Rudge turned down the Stoke manager's job several times, as he told BBC Radio Stoke: 'They asked me to be the manager, which I declined on two or three occasions. I didn't want to go from my sacking at Vale straight into the role at Stoke. I was flattered but it wasn't to be. I didn't intend any revenge on Vale by joining their local rivals. It was just the convenience of the area. My family and I are settled here, it was a quick opportunity to get back into football, and it was right for me at the time. I didn't want to move away from Stoke-on-Trent because the people here are the salt of the earth, I can relate to them, and I will always regard it as my home now after coming here in 1979.'

Incidentally, Rudge had actually scored *against* Port Vale as a player, in 1974 for Bristol Rovers. Still, it was only a consolation goal. No need to hold a grudge, Mr Rudge.

* * *

The story of John Rudge at Stoke City is an interesting one in itself. In his role, as he later described it, he would be 'involved in all aspects of the club, contracts, training and attending matches'. He joined in 1999 at one of the most interesting times in the club's history. He was initially working under Gary Megson and the Coates–Humphreys regime, having turned down the managerial hot seat himself, with Stoke still adapting to life in the third tier and at their new Britannia Stadium home. By November 1999, an Icelandic consortium completed a much-publicised and highly anticipated takeover of the club (you can read all about that in my other book – *Twinned with Reykjavik!*).

Shortly after the takeover, Megson was sacked, replaced by former Icelandic national manager Guðjón Thórdarson. Rudge's services, however, were retained, as his English league experience was invaluable to the incoming Icelanders. Thórdarson would often turn to Rudge for advice and suggestions for who to go after in the British transfer market, such as Scottish striker Chris Iwelumo, spotted at a game at Vale Park while on trial for Preston. Iwelumo said, 'We played Port Vale at Vale Park and beat them 3-1. I scored a goal, and the next morning, John Rudge, who had watched the game, offered me a contract at Stoke. I'd been at the Britannia Stadium all day with John Rudge; he offered me the contact, I went away to think about it and have some food, then came back and signed it. Preston offered a contract that evening after I'd signed. John Rudge was the main reason that I was there, and the relationship that Guðjón had with Rudge was great. Guðjón trusted John.'

Rudge's scouting wasn't just limited to UK shores. He was pivotal in bringing in Belarus international defender Sergei Shtanyuk and former Netherlands international winger Peter Hoekstra, widening Stoke's European footprint. The two signings were among the best pieces of business that the club had achieved in a long time, mainly thanks to the efforts of Rudge. He was also at the centre of some high-profile player departures, including Peter Thorne, Kris Commons and Ade Akinbiyi.

* * *

Rudge was again linked to the Stoke job following the departures of Thórdarson and, shortly afterwards, Steve Cotterill in 2002. He had turned down the caretaker position in May 2002, leaving it to Dave Kevan, before Tony Pulis took over the club for his first spell as manager. The former Vale boss worked well under Pulis, as the two men shared a lot of admiration and respect for each other. However, when Pulis was dismissed in the summer of 2005 by the Icelandic board for 'failing to exploit the foreign market', Rudge found himself working under a completely new character of a manager – another former Netherlands international, Johan Boskamp. The larger-than-life Dutchman was brought in by the Icelandic consortium to provide fresh impetus into the football being played on the pitch, and spearhead one last promotion bid to the Premier League promised land. The issue was that Boskamp had zero experience in English football, meaning any signings he made were unknown quantities, usually from the Belgian and Dutch leagues.

The First Division, now known as the Championship, has a long, demanding season, where, as the cliché goes, anyone can beat anyone. To approach a Championship season with a wealth of new unknown players from overseas would be a huge gamble, so proven domestic players were a necessity too. Rudge was tasked with finding such players and was able to bring in the likes of Bruce Dyer, Marlon Broomes, Peter Sweeney, Luke Chadwick and Paul Gallagher, to variable levels of success. Some may have been panic buys, as Boskamp wrestled with both the board and himself in pre-season. Rudge recalled, 'On our pre-season tour, Johan Boskamp talked of phoning the chairman and quitting the job. I had gladly worked night and day to help him get a team together that could compete in the Championship.' Boskamp said at the time, 'He [John Rudge] knows the game here in a way that I don't. Also, I don't have the patience to sit in an office.'

What started off as a fruitful relationship and a decent start to the season for Boskamp and Rudge descended into chaos after a night match at Coventry City's Ricoh Arena. During the game, Rudge came down from the directors' box to pass a note of advice on to Boskamp's assistant, Jan de Koning, with the manager occupied on the touchline. When the manager heard about the exchange he was furious, believing his staff were going behind his back and questioning both his ability and his authority. After Boskamp threatened to quit, both Rudge and de Koning were put on gardening leave, appeasing the boss until at least the end of the season. In February 2006, Boskamp said of the incident, 'If the players hadn't told me that John Rudge had come downstairs to tell a player what to do, I wouldn't have known anything. If Jesus Christ came downstairs to say "do this", I wouldn't care. I knew then that it was over. If I had said nothing, I would have lost all the respect of my players. Everybody says forgive; I can forgive, that is no problem. But I can't forget. Some people are disappointed, but it's got nothing to do with the club. It's between me, John and Jan. I said, "If you want John to stay with me or Jan to stay then it's not possible." If the club say John Rudge is more important than me then I really have no problem.'

The season went downhill soon after the Coventry incident, with many of Boskamp's imported signings failing to impress (or in some cases not even bothering to turn up at all). The capture of Paul Gallagher by Rudge was a good piece of business, keeping Stoke clear of the relegation zone thanks to numerous long-range goals and star performances. Reflecting on the incident and time spent with Boskamp, Rudge said, 'I had been involved with him [Boskamp] all the time he'd been at the club. In the dressing room discussing tactics and what have you. I'm in the dressing room at Coventry before the game. That's how close we were, and obviously you are there to try to help if you can. That's why I did what I did. During the game, we were having a bad spell. Their right-back was tearing down the flank without any opposition, so I thought we should bring somebody across from the other flank to sort it out. It was with about 20 minutes to go that I went down towards the dugout, which wasn't far from the directors' box at Coventry in those days. Boskamp was on the touchline, so I spoke instead to his assistant manager, Jan de Koning. But instead of Jan then speaking to Boskamp, he went straight to the touchline and shouted to the player himself. Ed de Goey was on the bench, and I gather he told Boskamp what had happened. Boskamp then thought me and Jan were conspiring behind his back. It wasn't like that, but I can see why he thought it was. I apologised the next day and said I was just trying to help.'

The good news for both Rudge and Stoke City in general was that in the summer of 2005, the Icelandic consortium sold the club back to Peter Coates, who had amassed his own personal fortune thanks to the success of bet365. Pulis was brought back as manager, meaning Rudge was back in the office instead of his (presumably now immaculately kept) garden. The flat-capped one said of his relationship with the club shop-capped one, 'I'm working with someone I get on really well with in Tony Pulis, and I hope that I can just help him by taking the strain off him because I know exactly what it's like to be a manager, which is a hard role, and can often be too much for one person. I'm here to lighten the load so he can focus on winning matches. My job involves 60 to 70 hours a week, it's very time-consuming.'

* * *

Rudge remained at Stoke until the end of the 2012/13 season, the Potters having gained promotion and maintained the Premier League status along the way. He left after 14 years with the club. In 2017 he returned to his beloved Port Vale to take up an advisory role, before becoming the club president in August 2019, where he remains at the time of writing. His spell at both clubs has made him something of a giant in Stoke-on-Trent football. When asked about where his loyalties lie, Vale or Stoke, Rudge diplomatically answered, 'I would just say I have been very fortunate and very proud to have served both clubs. I've been lucky to have enjoyed some really exciting times with both.' Many would recognise though that his impact on Port Vale stands unparalleled, and fans were delighted to have him back.

9

Cruel Britannia

BACK IN 1997, John Rudge's ever-extending scouting network at Port Vale was continuing to pluck players from the Dutch and Swedish leagues, bringing in Jan Jansson from IFK Norrköping and Mark Snijders from AZ Alkmaar. A little closer to home the club made their record signing, forking out £500,000 for curly haired winger Gareth Ainsworth from Lincoln City. Ainsworth would prove to be yet another shrewd signing by Rudge, being named player of the year in 1998 and moving on to the Premier League with Wimbledon for a highly profitable £2m.

The new signings at the start of the 1997/98 season were achievable thanks to a previous profitable player turnaround, as Jon McCarthy moved to Birmingham City for £1.5m having cost Vale £450,000 back in August 1995. The revolving-door transfer policy was a sign of the times at Vale Park. Having a footballing mind like Rudge was proving pivotal as the Valiants continued to punch above their weight in the second tier for a fourth successive season. Despite a promising preceding season, the upcoming goal was still survival.

Over in the temporary buildings and newly opened offices in and around the Britannia Stadium, Stoke's board moved to replace the outgoing Lou Macari by appointing his former assistant Chic Bates, with Peter Coates seemingly gambling on the cheap option after fan calls for experienced hands such as Sammy McIlroy and Denis Smith fell on deaf ears. Supporter resentment towards Coates and his boardroom associates was growing, but the move to the new stadium was a welcome distraction for the directors, despite the very obvious on-field issues that it was causing.

While Macari's departure had been sudden and unexpected, the transfer of top scorer Mike Sheron was less of a surprise. Sheron was sold in the summer to Queens Park Rangers for £2.75m, a fee that simply couldn't be turned down given the club's need for stadium funding. Sheron was chastised by fans for the move, but as with a lot of big-money transfers, there was more to the departure than met the eye. Sheron himself would later tell *Duck Magazine* that he didn't want to move, saying, 'We never seemed to be too well off financially and moving to the

Britannia Stadium at the time was a major move forward for the club. I accept that the bigger picture for the club was more important than keeping Mike Sheron at the club. This I found difficult to accept, but for the club's long-term planning a new stadium was essential.' Former Blackburn striker Peter Thorne was brought in for £550,000 to fill Sheron's metaphorically large boots.

Stoke's season kicked off in rather clumsy fashion, setting the tone for the months to follow. Queues and parking issues, ticketing problems, lack of running water and an underwhelming opening ceremony highlighted the teething problems with their new home. After a League Cup tie against Rochdale, which Stoke drew, the first league fixture at the Brit was against Swindon Town, which Stoke lost. Still, at least there were cheerleaders ('the City Slickers'), a brand-new hippo mascot ('Pottermus') and a Tom Jones lookalike. Having apparently learned nothing from Diana Ross's hilarious penalty miss during the 1994 World Cup opening ceremony, organisers asked Sir Stanley Matthews to score in front of the new North Stand. Sir Stan was 82, so it wasn't the biggest surprise when his shot failed to reach the goal. Dave Regis would have been proud.

As fans finally managed to find the right access roads and available parking spaces in order to get into the ground, the new stadium wasn't exactly feeling like home, and it took until 13 September 1997 for Stoke to finally find their first win in their new surroundings.

Vale's season had opened with two defeats but they had managed to pick up a few positive results by mid-September, including a 1-0 win at Crewe thanks to Lee Mills, in among the goals once again alongside Tony Naylor. The first Potteries derby at the Britannia Stadium fell on 12 October 1997, with the two teams separated by two places in the league by virtue of goals scored. The new setting seemed to breathe fresh life into the encounter as the first league clash of the season was an entertaining one, with 20,125 in attendance.

Kevin Keen was in inspired form for the home side, crossing for Richard Forsyth to head home from close range after just four minutes. Forsyth should have grabbed his second of the game soon after, having rounded ever-present Valiants goalkeeper Paul Musselwhite, but he somehow managed to shoot wide with the goal gaping. Following that, the visitors mounted their first meaningful attack of the game in the 21st minute when Rogier Koordes got the better of Ally Pickering to pick out Tony Naylor 15 yards from goal. The striker did remarkably well to get his head to the cross and equalise, giving Vale a much-needed foothold in the game.

The new found confidence for the visitors would soon cost them, though, as Stoke broke away thanks to a 60-yard run from influential midfielder Graham Kavanagh. The Irishman picked out Keen, who beat Musselwhite down low to the goalkeeper's right to restore the home side's lead.

The game kept moving at a frantic pace, and Vale were unlucky not to be level again just before half-time. Ainsworth was inches away with a header which was touched on to the crossbar by Muggleton, and Vale's subsequent penalty claims went unrewarded as defender Steve Tweed appeared to handle the ball in a scramble in the box, referee Clive Wilkes turning down the loud appeals. Instead the Valiants were rewarded with a corner, from which Ainsworth struck a far-post effort which was blocked on the line. A highly engaging first half, and the second half wasn't far off the same standard. Stoke thought they had a third when Forsyth's header was palmed away by Musselwhite, who seemed to do so with the ball already over the line, but no goal was given. Martin Foyle came off the bench to force a magnificent save out of Muggleton at the death, but Stoke held on for a well-earned victory. Potters fans were delighted, not only to pick up another win against their local rivals but to do so while securing victories in the last Potteries derby league game at the Vic and the first at the Brit.

* * *

The victory came at a time when Stoke were progressing nicely under Bates, and were sitting in the play-offs after a victory at Manchester City ten days later. The Potters even pulled off an impressive 3-0 win against Midlands rivals Wolverhampton Wanderers, who had brought a massive following to the Brit which had even spilt over from the South Stand into the Sentinel Stand. However, from mid-November, Stoke's season took a nosedive and they went ten games without a win, which included five straight losses. The first significant low point of the season came in the new year, when the Potters were beaten 7-0 by Birmingham City. The drubbing came just days after nine members of the squad had found out that they were to be transfer-listed, having discovered the news by reading it on the back page of *The Sentinel*. The result was the final straw for many supporters, whose anger towards the board had been growing for some time, and at the final whistle some 900 or so stormed the pitch, heading towards the West Stand where the directors were sat. Stewards and 100 police officers were deployed, along with horses and dogs, as 16 people were arrested. One fan was arrested outside the ground for stealing the match ball. Fans had been spilling on to the pitch from as early as the 56th minute, when none other than former Vale winger Jon McCarthy got himself on the scoresheet. The Britannia Stadium was starting to feel cursed.

Chic Bates was now a dead man walking, and City were a coffin on roller skates. After the humiliation, Bates said, 'It was a crushing defeat and an unbelievable scoreline, but it happened, and we've got to stand up and be counted. I feel pressure after a result like that, but we must now prepare for Tuesday's FA Cup tie at West Brom. The lads are down and it's my job to lift them. As for the fans, they are football enthusiasts and want to see a winning team. When the score gets out of hand like that you can see their reaction.'

Stoke would actually win their next league game, beating Bradford 2-1 in front of the Sky Sports cameras, but the writing was on the wall for Bates, who was sacked but would still remain on the coaching staff. Yet another example of a long list of poor decisions from the higher-ups. Peter Coates would step down as chairman amid the protests, and former Potters player Chris Kamara was brought in as the new manager with the unenviable task of turning fortunes and steering the club away from relegation.

Over in the north of the city, things weren't panning out any better. Vale went on a horrendous losing streak from the end of November to mid-January of seven in a row, part of a run which saw only one victory in 15. Goals were drying up and the reliance on

Mills and Naylor to constantly produce the goods was catching up with Rudge's team. Their run of defeats was actually ended by a highly spirited 0-0 draw at Highbury in the FA Cup third round against Arsène Wenger's Arsenal, followed by a 1-1 draw after extra time in the replay at Vale Park. Former Stoke defender Lee Dixon missed his penalty, but the Gunners ran out 4-3 winners in the shoot-out and would go on to win the trophy. The strong performances against an Arsenal side which included David Seaman, Dennis Bergkamp, Patrick Vieira, Ian Wright, Ray Parlour and Marc Overmars would give Vale a much-needed confidence boost going into the final run-in.

By the second Potteries derby meeting, on 1 March 1998, both teams were in the mire. The Valiants were in the relegation zone and two points from safety, while the Potters were one position and one point better off. The situation was a far cry from the hugely anticipated top-of-the-table clash of March 1993, albeit in a higher division. This was evident from the attendance – 13,853, the lowest crowd for a Football League Potteries derby since 1931.

There was one similarity for the visitors from that 1993 clash. Once again, Stoke were debuting a moustachioed former top goalkeeper of European football who had joined on loan from Merseyside, this time the robust shot stopper Neville Southall, arriving from Everton. This was my first personal visit to Vale Park too. We were in the side stand for the Sunday afternoon clash. I was only ten, and I couldn't really see much, but I don't think I missed much either. The game was contested as a 'must not lose' rather than a 'must win', and both sides put their emphasis on defence rather than attack, a stark contrast from the prior high-octane meeting at the Britannia Stadium.

Martin Foyle went close early on for the home side, bringing out a brave block from Stoke's Icelandic international defender Larus Sigurdsson. Peter Thorne, possibly Stoke's only bright spark of the season, went close for the visitors, but the first half showed why both teams were struggling at the wrong end of the table. The game descended into a feisty affair, with a first-half tussle in front of the dugout between opposing players and a knee-high challenge from Jansson going unpunished. Jansson would then go close to opening the scoring, followed by Ainsworth spawning the best chance of the game after rounding Southall, but neither team were able to break the deadlock and it finished 0-0. Angela Smith summed up the entertainment on show, 'I distinctly remember the game in March 1998 away. We were living in North Berwick, Scotland, and although I used to travel the four hours 20 minutes back for home games, this time I persuaded my husband to join me. He is no stranger to local rivalry being a Hibernian fan. Imagine my disappointment when after all my "bigging up" of the occasion it was a pretty dull goalless draw. I have witnessed some great battles over the years, but this was not one of the better ones. He was unimpressed and has not attended one of these games since.'

Not an altogether pleasing result for either side, who had both lost their ability to win games. But the point could still be crucial by the end of the season for one of the two teams.

* * *

After yet another defeat on the road, Chris Kamara resigned as Stoke manager, jumping before he was pushed. The man who is nowadays better known for his *Soccer Saturday* antics had arrived with bold claims of taking the 'sleeping monster' Stoke to the Premier League, but was dismissed having won just one of his 14 games in charge. Assistant manager Alan Durban was appointed caretaker until the end of the season. Vice-chairman Keith Humphreys described Kamara's tenure as 'a nightmare'.

Vale found a bit of form in March, including back-to-back wins against fellow strugglers Reading and Manchester City, but with six games remaining both Potteries teams were fighting for their lives. It would all go down to the final game of the season.

Port Vale would go to Huddersfield Town, backed by 4,000 travelling supporters at the McAlpine Stadium; Stoke would host Manchester City in a hostile clash in front of 26,664. The game at the Britannia Stadium is burned into my memory. Judgement Day was upon us.

Reading had already been relegated going into the final day, so there were two places to be filled by two of Vale, Portsmouth, Manchester City and Stoke. Vale were in 20th on 46 points, level on points and goal difference with Portsmouth in 21st. In the drop zone, Stoke were also on 46 points, but with an inferior goal difference, and Manchester City were in 23rd on 45, with by far the best goal difference of the four struggling clubs. John Rudge's side needed a win to ensure survival, having lost their previous three games. Prior to the match, Vale's star signing Gareth Ainsworth was full of positivity, declaring, 'We will go to Huddersfield on the last day in good spirits – there's still a buzz about the dressing room. We've just played four top teams and now against a middle-of-the-road team we will be on fire to get the points. I would like to think that when that final whistle goes next week, I'm still a Division One player. We have to be up for such a do-or-die game. I think it will be one of the biggest-ever games for this club. Our supporters have been brilliant and hopefully we can justify their support next week.'

The two games couldn't have started with much more contrasting emotions for the respective sets of supporters. At Huddersfield, the Valiants took the lead after just 114 seconds with the 35-year-old Martin Foyle the hero once again. At the Britannia, the menacing atmosphere had been threatening to boil over since fans had started to arrive. It was no secret that Manchester City supporters had been buying tickets for the home end in the lead-up to the encounter, and the stretch from Stoke train station up Campbell Road had resembled a war zone before kick-off. Two minutes into the televised game, around the same time that the Vale fans were celebrating their opening goal, fighting began to break out all across the Sentinel Stand, with dozens of visiting supporters taking to the pitch and charging across towards the safe haven of the South Stand where the away fans were packed in and willing to receive them. The game was temporarily halted, as it would be throughout the first half, as violent clashes were erupting in several parts of the home end. Peter Thorne would even later say, 'I'm from Manchester myself, and on one occasion someone I knew growing up actually ran past me on the pitch. I kept my head down. The last thing I wanted was for someone to shout out, "All right, Thorney!"' When the match eventually did play out, it was the visitors looking like the only team fighting for their lives. The Citizens controlled the opening 20 minutes with only a brief flurry from the Potters giving Thorne the home side's sole early opportunity.

By 3.24pm, Vale were in full control of their match up in Yorkshire. After Musselwhite had kept out Lee Richardson's effort for the mid-table Terriers, Ainsworth received the ball upfield to cross for Foyle, who flicked on to Jan Jansson to bury his first-time effort and double Vale's lead. Some five minutes later, back at the Brit, Shaun Goater broke through the Swiss cheese Stoke defence to open the scoring and trigger yet more disorder in the stands. At half-time the writing was more or less on the wall for the Potters, and the Valiants were 45 minutes away from safety. Jansson's clever free kick put the game beyond doubt at Huddersfield, while goals from Paul Dickov and Lee Bradbury either side of a Peter Thorne consolation piled on the misery for Alan Durban and Stoke. Another goal from The Goat made it 4-1 on 70 minutes, before Thorne got his second of the day.

By the time the fifth Manchester City goal had gone in, a lot of Stoke fans had gone home. Those who remained tried to see the funny side of things, singing 'we'll see you all next year' to the Man City faithful as their club was also falling through the trap door thanks to results elsewhere. Portsmouth were on their way to a 3-1 win at Bradford, and Vale were 4-0 up at the McAlpine as Lee Mills capped off a fine individual scoring season to head home after yet more great play from Jansson. The Vale fans were in party mode, safe in the knowledge that they were staying up in style, but Stoke were going down with a whimper and a 5-2 loss. John Rudge and chairman Bill Bell took to the field at full time to celebrate with the supporters, as players flung their shirts into the bouncing away end.

The day had started with the hopes of both sets of fans that their team would stand up and fight for their lives. The Valiants were clearly ready to do that, echoed by Ainsworth's pre-match rally. The impressive Jansson also showed he was committed to the cause, later saying, 'That's the first time in my career that I haven't been able to sleep before a game. In Sweden you play almost for fun, but here this is my work and it was important we stayed up.' Rudge reflected, 'I would like to thank the chairman and his board of directors because they have stuck with me through difficult times and now it's paid dividends. The players and myself would also like to thank the supporters for being so tremendous with us during this season's ups and downs. They have stuck with us through the bad times and that has been a big factor. We made our season a lot more exciting than it should have been, but the players were simply magnificent when it mattered most.'

The mood couldn't have been more different in ST4. Manchester City had gone down, but at least they had shown some spirit, and gave their fans something to cheer despite falling to the third tier for the first time in their history. Stoke just didn't turn up, which was upsetting for caretaker manager Durban: 'That was the most disappointing thing, our performance on the day was so poor. It was as bad as getting relegated because the stadium was full. I thought we let everyone down very badly and that hurts me, although in a funny sort of way to have won today and still gone down would probably have hurt more. We started fairly poorly and never really recovered from that. We have conceded too many goals with balls over the top this season and it was in evidence again. We kept trying to play offside, but that is defenders abdicating their responsibilities and we are not very good at playing it.'

Stoke's on-loan goalkeeper Neville Southall looked back on his time at the club in the lowest possible terms. He wrote in his autobiography, 'We lost 5-2 and went down with Man City. Port Vale, Stoke's big rivals but who they dwarfed in size, stayed up by a single point. I'm sure it must have been one of the darkest days in the club's history. Afterwards nobody spoke to me at all. I gathered my things and left and never went back. One of the worst episodes of my life had drawn to a close.' Reflecting on some of the performances and club decisions, Southall also stated, 'Players just didn't perform, and I know I didn't play very well. Chris [Kamara] was having a bad time at home and his father died around this time. But there was no sympathy from the Stoke board and he resigned at the start of April before they could sack him. He had been in charge for just ten weeks. I think the lack of empathy and sympathy was one of the most disgraceful things I've ever witnessed in football.'

The day finished with Port Vale in 19th position, on 49 points, well deserving of their First Division status. For Stoke, it was 23rd and the dreaded (R) stamp. The fans had shown more fight than the players, with 15 arrests (ten during the game). The Potters were in crisis, on and off the pitch. The glory days of the Victoria Ground and Lou Macari's famous teams were feeling like a distant memory. City had taken four points from Vale during the season, but there was no doubt that the Valiants were once again feeling like the dominant team in Stoke-on-Trent. The next time the two teams would meet, the situation at Stoke City would be very different.

10

Norse Code

AFTER MANY years of bravely battling against the drop, Port Vale were finally relegated from the First Division in the 1999/2000 season, meaning that going into the new millennium they would be reunited with their city rivals. Brian Horton was now their manager, and club mainstays Martin Foyle, Paul Musselwhite and Ian Bogie had all departed. The financial situation at Vale Park was nothing short of dire, with more and more fan protests against chairman Bill Bell occurring on a regular basis. Work on the development of the Lorne Street Stand ground to a halt due to the lack of money to complete the project, leaving a constant concrete reminder of the club's plight. Bell was quick to stress that the club was not on the verge of collapse or liquidation, insisting he was 'having ongoing talks with potential investors who have a football background, and as always, if they're prepared to take

Port Vale forward, I am willing to sell some of my shares'.

There were growing concerns however, and by September 2000 the latest (but ultimately not the last) rumours of a takeover-cum-merger with Stoke City were floating around the six towns There had been reports a year earlier that a possible collapse of the initial Icelandic deal to take over Stoke had prompted Bell to call up the group to try to lure the investors up the road to Vale Park. However, the mere suggestion of a merger with their deadly rivals had Bell scrambling to shoot down the story, 'Our fans would sooner see me shut the gates permanently than go in with Stoke. Like all businesses, we will survive by operating day to day. There'll be no need to go in with Stoke, thankyou very much.' Shutting the gates was looking more and more like a realistic possibility, and for many fans, the desperate need for both financial support for the club and protection against mergers and ground shares was enough to begin the first steps in establishing a consortium that would later come to be known as Valiant 2001, intent on achieving ownership of the club a couple of years later.

Stoke, starting their first full season under the ownership of the Icelandic-run parent company Stoke Holding SA and with Guðjón Thórdarson in charge, were feeling positive and optimistic about the season ahead. They had kicked off life under the Icelandic regime in style, winning the Auto Windscreens Shield at Wembley and making the play-off semi-finals, as well as bringing in a raft of Norsemen from all across Scandinavia. After their play-off heartbreak, Stoke were looking to go one better in 2000/01. They had started the season well, losing only one of their opening six games, as Thórdarson's Icelandic imports settled into Second Division life nicely. Despite a couple of back-to-back 3-0 home wins, Vale had started the season poorly, but Tony Naylor was back among the goals, as was new signing Marc Bridge-Wilkinson.

The first Potteries derby was on a Sunday afternoon on 17 September 2000 at Vale Park. With the situation very different from their previous trip to Burslem, Stoke fans were in a cheerful mood. The old Rudge chants had been replaced with 'he's red, he's white, he hates the Vale sh*te, Johnny Rudge, Johnny Rudge!'. The Port Vale board's decision to allocate only 4,500 tickets to Stoke fans was looking short-sighted, as the visitors could have probably brought twice that number. The overall attendance of 8,948 meant that the board had essentially left money on the table, not something they could afford to do. The game would not feature a single local-born player in either team, but despite this, it was still an entertaining and strongly contested clash. Vale even had their own Nordic striker on the team sheet in Finnish target-man Ville Viljanen. Stoke's 16-man squad included three Icelanders, a Swede and a Dane.

The first Potteries derby for three seasons started at a frantic pace, with two goals in the opening 15 minutes. Bridge-Wilkinson, who had arrived at Vale on a free transfer from Derby County, put the home side ahead early on with a header from Matty Carragher's cross. While Vale fans were revelling in their early lead, Stoke came out strong after the restart with Graham Kavanagh delivering a pinpoint cross to find Bermudian Kyle Lightbourne, whose powerful header was kept out by Mark Goodlad. From the resulting corner, Lightbourne fired Stoke level after Kavanagh had picked out Nicky Mohan, whose effort could only be parried. Stoke then twice hit the bar through Lightbourne and on-loan striker Marvin Robinson. Midway through the first half, Tony Naylor struck out at Stoke's record signing, Brynjar Gunnarsson, resulting in a booking, but Thórdarson would later insist that the card should have been red.

Vale threatened the visitors' goal with two approaches that would later become synonymous with the Potters – a long-range effort from Dave Brammer, and a barrage of long throws. Though there was no winner, Stoke fans were rewarded with the return of their main goal threat Peter Thorne in the second half, making his first appearance of the season after

167

injury. The draw kept their unbeaten run going into a fourth game and would keep the Potters challenging at the top. For the Valiants, the point formed part of a seven-game run without a win in the league; they were struggling to adapt to life in the Second Division.

* * *

Stoke maintained their consistent form right up to the second Potteries derby of the season, at the Britannia Stadium on 17 February 2001. Vale were still struggling, having had a poor Christmas run that included four defeats on the bounce. They had also been humiliated by non-league side Canvey Island in the FA Cup, losing 2-1 in a replay following a highly entertaining 4-4 draw down in Essex. Around the same time, Stoke had also been humiliated in both domestic cups, losing to non-league Nuneaton Borough in the FA Cup and then being hammered 8-0 at home to Liverpool in the League Cup.

A home win against Bournemouth prior to the meeting at the Brit was a confidence boost for the Valiants. The Potters were also buoyant following a 4-0 win away at Peterborough. Kick-off was moved forward three hours by the police to a high-noon showdown at Trentham Lakes. The crowd of 22,133 was the highest attended Potteries derby since the Autoglass Trophy clash way back in 1993, as Stoke fans were enjoying another promotion-chasing season under Thórdarson.

Once again the game started at a frantic pace, with the visitors earning a corner in the first minute, Bridge-Wilkinson's delivery headed over and wide by Onandi Lowe. Stoke's giant Icelandic forward Ríkharður Daðason then went close for the home side, heading Tony Dorigo's cross into the waiting arms of Mark Goodlad. After both teams were wasteful in possession in central midfield, Lowe got his foot on the ball high upfield for Vale, playing in Tony Naylor who sold the dummy to cut inside and move the ball on to his right foot, before hitting a low shot that looked destined to settle in the net at the near post but was turned behind by Birkir Kristinsson. As two minutes of added time were announced at the end of the first half, Naylor again escaped the attentions of the Stoke defence. The forward poked the ball away from Kristinsson and seemed certain to score, but his effort was heroically blocked by Brynjar Gunnarsson.

Ten minutes into the second half, the deadlock was broken by the home side. More good work down the left by Dorigo led to a deep cross that was headed in by Irish midfielder James O'Connor. It was now Vale's turn to search for an equaliser, going close with a deep header from Michael Cummins which just went wide of the post.

With ten minutes remaining the Valiants hit Stoke on the counter-attack after a free kick was cleared upfield to Naylor. The striker checked his run with two defenders on him, playing an inch-perfect ball to the advancing Dave Brammer. The midfielder took one touch before unleashing an unstoppable finish from the edge of the penalty area to bring Vale level to the delight of the 2,000-plus Vale fans at the far end of the stadium. Stoke pushed for a winner, with Goodfellow bringing a good save out of Goodlad, and Mohan struck the post from the resultant corner. It ended all square, both teams content with the point.

After the final whistle, Guðjón Thórdarson commented, 'Vale worked harder than us from the start. That's why we hardly had a kick for 15 minutes. Too many of our players thought others would do their job for them.' His Port Vale counterpart Brian Horton said, 'I was proud of my players today, I thought we played some really good stuff. We started the game off very well, we set off about it right. The keeper [Kristinsson] made a fantastic save off [Naylor], normally Naylor would bend that across him to the far post, but he tried to do him with the eyes, and bent it to the near post. For Naylor's second chance, the defender [Gunnarsson] has come from nowhere to block it. I think it would have been a travesty if we hadn't got a point out of today. I thought it was a great derby game, great atmosphere, lovely stadium, and we've more than matched them.' Dave Brammer echoed those sentiments, saying, 'I think both sets of fans were brilliant, it was a great atmosphere.'

The draw was the second positive result for Vale in a row, and part of a run of 12 games unbeaten which saw them move away from any lingering relegation danger.

* * *

Stoke and Vale would meet again that season in the LDV Vans Trophy. The competition was the rebranded Auto Windscreens Shield, once upon a time the Autoglass Trophy and several other incarnations. Much like in their 1993 meeting in the Autoglass, Stoke were the current holders of the trophy. The tie was set for Vale Park in February but it was postponed, not once but twice, first due to frost and then due to waterlogging, meaning there would be no repeat of the ball getting stuck in the mud. The Football League had run out of patience with the cash-strapped Valiants and switched the tie to the Britannia Stadium. It was a decision which had upset Vale manager Horton, but it was out of the club's hands. Horton put out his best 11 while Thórdarson rested several key players, with the promotion run-in hotting up. The crowd was demonstrably down, with little notice and limited interest in the competition resulting in an attendance of only 11,323, though that was still more than twice as many as the previous LDV Vans tie for Stoke at home to Walsall.

Tackles went in thick and fast in a lively opening salvo for both teams. Kavanagh warmed the hands of Goodlad on a chilly night with a tame effort from distance early on, while Vale continued to test the Potters with long throws. Sagi Burton headed wide from one such Michael Walsh throw. Naylor and Brammer were linking up again to good effect, and Micky Cummins brought a low save out of Kristinsson in the first half. As with the first 45, Vale were looking the more likely to score in the second half, and Cummins broke the deadlock for the visitors when Stoke failed to clear a cross from the left. Cummins struck the loose ball first time into the bottom corner in front of the Boothen End.

Burton again went close, rattling the crossbar with a header, but this time it was Stoke who struck a late equaliser as a high ball forward into the Vale box bounced around before falling to Nicky Mohan, who lashed home from eight yards out in the 87th minute to force extra time at the Brit. Mohan celebrated in front of the away end by showing the travelling supporters the Stoke badge on his shirt. Extra time would be contested under golden goal rules, essentially meaning it was sudden death – first goal wins it, otherwise we would go to penalties. Vale were looking more likely, mounting pressure on the Stoke back line, and when Naylor beat two men on the touchline he worked his way into the penalty area. His low drag-back was blocked by Mohan using his hand, and the referee awarded a penalty. Defender Mohan had gone from hero to villain for the Potters.

Marc Bridge-Wilkinson picked up the ball; if he scored, Vale were through. He beat Kristinsson down to the goalkeeper's right, winning the tie, as the Vale bench stormed across the pitch to celebrate in front of the elated away fans, the charge led by Horton. Tom from the *Ale and the Vale* podcast cites the penalty as a personal highlight following the Valiants in the Potteries derby, recalling, 'I just remember being told before the game that he had a bruised toe, but the keeper still got nowhere near!'

It was jubilation for the Vale fans behind that goal. For Stoke fans, however, a frustrating night, not least myself. I kicked a chair in anger at full time, sending a chunk of plastic flying down about ten rows. Thankfully no one saw it, or I might have received a ban! While the memories of the on-field Valiant celebrations aren't particularly fond for myself, Kirsty from the *Ale and the Vale* podcast calls what happened a personal highlight: 'I remember Brian Horton running over to the Vale fans, punching the air. Brilliant!'

Podcast co-host Dan also recounts the game as one of his favourites, 'I was still at school at the time, and I begged my dad to take me. He said we couldn't go as there was likely to be trouble. Then about two hours before kick-off, he told me to go get ready, we were off to the match! I remember the excitement of being able to go, then when we scored the golden goal and the away end erupted, that moment will live with me forever. The Vale fans got kept behind after, and I remember Naylor and Bridge-Wilkinson coming out to warm down. The away end started chanting again, and the stewards made them go back up the tunnel!'

There were a number of similarities between the 1993 Autoglass Trophy and the 2001 LDV Vans Trophy derbies. Once again we were at the regional section semi-final, and Stoke were the home team (albeit by acts of God in 2001). Stoke were the holders for both ties, with one eye on promotion when the March clashes came around. Vale ran out winners by one goal on both occasions and would go on to win the trophy in both 1993 and in 2001. Vale celebrated victory at Cardiff's Millennium Stadium on 22 April, beating Brentford 2-1 in the final thanks to goals from Marc Bridge-Wilkinson and Steve Brooker.

Their superb second-half-of-the-season turnaround saw Horton's men lose just once in 21, which even gave them a faint sniff of the play-offs, but the LDV

Vans Trophy and day out in Cardiff would make for a welcome prize in the end.

At the end of the season, Horton reflected on the LDV meeting, saying, 'In the end they had to switch the tie, which we didn't want to do, I wanted to win that game and it puts pressure on us to go down there. But we played fantastic and thoroughly deserved to win the game, culminating with us winning the LDV at Cardiff. To beat Stoke on the way was a nice one for our fans.' Horton's assistant, Mark Grew, recalled the moment of the golden goal, saying, 'He [Horton] said he hadn't got much pace, but that night he had, that was for sure! It was a great occasion to beat Stoke, and to go there and win in the style we did was exceptional.' Golden goal scorer Bridge-Wilkinson reflected, 'I was lucky enough to have the chance to put the goal in, but it was a team performance that got us that far. Looking back, we perhaps could have won it in normal time, which didn't happen, but we still got to the final anyway. I was always going to take the penalty. I didn't even feel nervous really. I was ecstatic that we had got the penalty, I ran up and grabbed the ball and I was buzzing like the rest of the lads. Then I suddenly realised that I needed to calm myself and take it. I took a minute to myself and had a wander, trying to compose myself, then stuck it in the net. I did a live radio interview two or three days afterwards; I was more nervous doing the interview than I was taking the penalty!'

* * *

Stoke fans were hoping that there would be one more similarity to 1992/93, which ended in promotion for the Potters. In 2000/01 Stoke's bid for automatic promotion stuttered after the league draw and cup loss to Vale, meaning the season ended with yet more play-off heartache, this time crumbling at the Bescot Stadium as Walsall ran out 4-2 winners. There was an end-of-season post-mortem at the Britannia Stadium, with managerial and boardroom squabbles that nearly ended in the dismissal of Guðjón Thórdarson, but he was to be given one more season to achieve promotion. Vale carried their league and LDV Vans momentum up to May 2001, but their season ended with a bit of a whimper, unable to manage a win from any of their final three games. They finished 11th, a position that had looked nigh-on impossible a few months earlier with the team struggling in the relegation zone. It was also yet another good season for the Valiants in the Potteries derby encounters, drawing the two league games and winning in the LDV Vans Trophy. Unfortunately, matters off the pitch were not showing any signs of improvement, as the club was heading for administration.

* * *

By the summer of 2001, both teams were dealing with their own respective monetary issues. Things were not quite so desperate at Stoke but the Icelandic board had reached the end of their financial rope with the manager and fellow countryman Thórdarson. Graham Kavanagh, the man who had become a vital part of the midfield since his move in 1996, was sold to Stoke's other rivals at the time, Cardiff City, for £1m.

Not long later, the main goal-getter and crowd favourite Peter Thorne was also sold to Cardiff. Speaking to *Duck Magazine* in October 2019, Thorne recalled, 'It all came to a head when I was called to a meeting with John Rudge. It was just us two in a room. He basically told me the club had to sell me because they needed the money. I was gutted. I did everything to stay but from that moment, I had little choice. £1.7m was a lot of cash back then.'

Brian Horton was also looking to balance the books, relying on free transfer arrivals such as Rae Ingram, Ian Armstrong and Stephen McPhee to strengthen the squad. Horton told the club's website, 'Finances play a big part in football now. It's a situation as managers where you can't win because you don't want to sell your better players. But at the end of the day, the club has to survive financially, and we are finding it difficult at the moment, for various reasons.'

* * *

Both teams started the new season with two wins from their opening three games, but while Stoke carried their good form on through the autumn months Vale tailed off. When they met at Vale Park on 21 October 2001, Stoke were once again flying high in the play-off positions while Vale had settled into mid-table. The crowd of 10,344 was an improvement on the previous season's attendance, again the highest home gate of the season, though the empty seats in the closed Railway Paddock made for a sad sight (and a sad site, in the case of the building site at the Lorne Street Stand) on the hard camera.

Stoke's continental side made a promising start, but Vale were quick to close down the space. A shot from just inside the Stoke area from Ian Armstrong brought a good save out of Neil Cutler at his near post as Vale mounted the pressure in the first half. Steve Brooker was posing a constant threat too for the home team but the first half finished 0-0. In the second half, a loose pass from Peter Hoekstra presented the ball to Armstrong, who made a forward pass that cut through the Stoke defence to play in McPhee, but Stoke were again grateful to Cutler, who denied the Vale top scorer one-on-one.

The Valiants eventually did take the lead after some nice build-up play presented Brooker with the ball on the right. His cross was too good for the Stoke defence and Stephen McPhee was able to head home to the delight of the home fans behind the goal. With 20 minutes to go, Stoke were still struggling to create chances. Andy Cooke got his head on Clive Clarke's cross from the left but couldn't direct it goalwards. With just over ten minutes remaining, an inspired double change from Thórdarson resulted in the equaliser. Substitute Lewis Neal played a forward ball which found its way through to the other replacement, Chris Iwelumo. The big Scot rounded keeper Goodlad to slot home and celebrate with the away fans spilling on to the side of the pitch. Stoke had a late chance to win it and Cooke was presented with two opportunities to snatch a second goal, but he spurned them both. Vale also looked to snatch it with pressure from a couple of late corners, but it was again honours even and chants of 'You'll never beat the Vale!'

Stoke goalscorer Iwelumo, originally spotted at Vale Park and signed by John Rudge of all people, recounted his Potteries derby goal: 'One of my closest friends, Sagi Burton, was the centre-back for Vale that day. We were signed around the same time – him for Port Vale and me for Stoke. We are still very close today and I still banter him because he was marking me. I never really knew how big the rivalry was until after I scored that goal. I never ripped up trees for

Stoke but the fans have always been very appreciative and held me in high regard, as I do for them, because of goals like that. The Port Vale goal, when you look at what it meant and who it was against, is up there as my best goal.'

Ale and the Vale podcast co-host Dan recalls the equaliser and subsequent fallout as a particular personal Port Vale-supporting low point, 'I remember Chris Iwelumo scoring and then fans starting fighting, as some Stoke fans were sitting in the home end. The atmosphere turned very hostile after that.'

Though the point at Vale Park was a useful one to Stoke, and they were happy to take something away with them after falling behind, it hadn't escaped anyone's attentions that they were now five Potteries derbies without a win, their last victory coming in the first derby clash at the Britannia Stadium. With the exception of the LDV Vans Trophy victory in extra time, each of their four league meetings since 1998 had ended in a draw, the last three ending 1-1. Even the LDV Vans tie was 1-1 after 90 minutes. The Potteries derby matches were proving to be tight contests, as they had been ever since the reuniting of the two sides in 1989. Of the 19 encounters between the two Stoke-on-Trent sides since then, only two had finished with a win by more than one goal.

* * *

Stoke's good form continued through to the turn of the year, only broken up by a 6-1 thumping at Wigan, their one defeat in 19 outings. Vale's form remained inconsistent through the Christmas period but they managed to find the winning touch once again in 2002. The return clash at the Britannia Stadium was on 10 February. An impressive 23,019 were in attendance as Stoke chased promotion and Vale hoped to deal yet another blow to their bitter rivals. Vale set the tempo right from the kick-off, McPhee winning his early battle with Sergei Shtanyuk, before Marc Bridge-Wilkinson played in Brooker, drawing a full-stretch save out of Cutler. Bridge-Wilkinson should have put the visitors ahead when a cross went all the way across the six-yard box, but his outstretched boot could only steer the ball wide with the goal gaping. Brooker went close again with a powerful shot from the edge of the area, before Shtanyuk headed wide for the home side from a corner.

Vale took a deserved first-half lead in scrappy fashion. A long throw from Matty Carragher on 36 minutes was met by Shtanyuk, but the giant Belarusian could only head it on to the back of Michael Cummins' head. The rebound looped into the far corner of the net, seemingly in slow motion as Cummins, not fully aware of what had transpired, wheeled away in celebration. The goalscorer was still somewhat confused and disorientated as he ran away from the away end to celebrate with team-mates.

Vale didn't let up and were looking more like the side chasing promotion. Carragher was causing problems down the right, and McPhee hit the bar, all occurring in the first half. Stoke were better in the second period, putting pressure on the Vale back line with corners, free kicks and long throws of their own. As Stoke corner-taker Bjarni Guðjónsson, son of the manager Guðjón Thórdarson, went across to take the set pieces, he was met with chants of 'Daddy's boy' from the Vale fans.

Stoke couldn't offer enough for an equaliser, and Vale defended resolutely to hold on for victory. Brian Horton was again kissing the air in front of the away end. The celebrations continued long after the final whistle, with Vale fans ripping out and tossing red chairs as they eventually departed the South Stand. It certainly wasn't a fluke victory and in the end the scoreline probably flattered Stoke.

After the game, Horton said, 'I knew we would put on a show because we were ready for it from training, but you still have to prove it out there. Our first-half performance was tremendous, the game should have been over at half-time. That was a tremendous team display. I'm proud of our supporters and players today, it's a magnificent result for all of us.' Assistant Mark

Grew echoed his manager's words, 'When we came in at half-time, we felt disappointed in a sense. We thought the game should have been over, but at 1-0, we all know it never is. The keeper Cutler has made two or three really good saves early doors for Brooker I think, and if those goals go in, it seals the game. Second half I thought we defended very well, they hardly had a kick at our goal.' Goalscorer Cummins, who admitted that he didn't know much about the goal and initially thought someone else had stuck the ball in, said, 'It was just a brilliant, brilliant, brilliant game, brilliant atmosphere, everything's electric. You feel the energy from the crowd, really urging you to win. Brilliant.' Yes, it was five brilliants for Vale. For Stoke, it was more of the same sobering feeling of falling short against their bitter rivals.

By the February 2001 loss, there was a feeling among the Stoke fans that, despite having the more expensive, better-positioned league team, the players just weren't up for the Potteries derby in the same way that their Port Vale counterparts were. The perception was that Horton was capable of getting his more limited squad of British players more motivated for the derby than Thórdarson was with his assembled mass of continental players. Chris Iwelumo, who didn't start in the game despite his goal at Vale Park earlier in the season, would discuss that topic in *Twinned with*

Reykjavik, saying, 'I think every footballer goes into a match to win it, but I think that rivalry had that bit of an edge that the British players understood. They're in and around the area, they read the newspapers, they speak with the fans, whereas I think the Scandinavians stayed with their families, not mixing with the community. The Vale players got that extra 15 per cent because of the atmosphere around the place. The build-up to the game, every time you go out for dinner, everyone spoke about it, "Are we going to get the win?" I don't think the Scandinavian players mixed in that environment, so the build-up may have been a little bit different for them.'

* * *

Boy, that was a tough chapter for a Stoke fan like myself! Those years, 2000 to 2002, were essentially slap bang in the middle of my high school years at St Thomas More in Longton. For most of that time I was sat next to a devoted Vale fan, Nick Engleman, in registration, so the grief I had to endure on at least two occasions wasn't much fun, and in all honesty, the three draws weren't exactly anything for a Stoke fan to shout about either. The good news for fans like myself was that Stoke would go on to seal promotion in dramatic style that season, overcoming Cardiff City in the play-off semi-finals thanks to a memorable win at Ninian Park, followed up by a comfortable 2-0 win over Brentford in the final at the Millennium Stadium. The play-off jinx was broken for the Potters, but the derby jinx would endure, to this day of writing.

11

Keeping a Safe Distance

A LOT of time has passed since that last league meeting between the two Potteries sides in February 2002. A lot has happened to the two clubs too, and though their on-field encounters might have come to a halt there were still some off-field clashes, and for once I'm not talking about the fans.

Soon after the two clubs parted ways in the league, the collapse of ITV Digital left many clubs in deep financial peril, not least Port Vale. The Burslem club lost £400,000 in the collapse, while racking up debts of £2.4m and annual losses of £500,000, eventually entering administration. The desperation to secure funds to keep the club afloat led administrators to the doors of Robbie Williams, hoping the multi-millionaire pop star and childhood Vale fan would bail them out. However, help was not yet forthcoming from Williams, as administrator Bob Young explained: 'I don't think that we can rely on there being some saviour out there who's suddenly going to pump hundreds of thousands, or millions of pounds into this club. Being where we are, everyone talks about Robbie Williams. I have got a letter through to Robbie in Los Angeles. He knows this club's for sale, but I don't think we should rely on the fact that he's going to bail us out.' The singer had recently celebrated signing a new record deal with EMI worth up to £80m by famously declaring, 'I'm rich beyond my wildest dreams!' However, Williams' management company IE Music would confirm that the former Take That star 'will not be one of the investors in Port Vale'. Williams would become a majority shareholder in the club in later years, and even played a large concert at Vale Park in 2022.

The news back in 2003 wasn't all bad for Vale fans, as stories of up to four bidders for the club were released by the administrators. The only problem, and it was a big problem, was that the fourth anonymous bid was, in all likelihood, coming from Stoke Holding SA. Yes, the Icelandic owners of Stoke City were once again circling Vale Park like vultures around carrion. In early 2003, Stoke chairman Gunnar Gíslason had stoked the fires (excuse the phrasing) by saying that a club merger would make 'financial sense' and pointed to the 'economies of scale' of ground-sharing. Gíslason said, 'People are forgetting that Port Vale is in administration and football is in crisis. Administration is being used in football not to pay creditors, which is bad business and ethically wrong. Ground-sharing makes financial sense and soon football will have to face reality.' Administrator Young would add, 'The financial merits of having only one football ground in Stoke-on-Trent are overwhelming and it makes perfect financial sense for any new owners of Port Vale to sell Vale Park to a property developer and negotiate a ground-share agreement with Stoke City.'

Young seemed happy to discuss the rumours, without confirming or denying them, 'I have received four offers for Port Vale. Three parties have gone public and none of them is Stoke City. I have also received an offer from a London solicitor on behalf of a client who has insisted on anonymity. I cannot confirm whether that is or is not anything to do with Stoke Holding SA. I am aware Stoke City have issued a statement saying they have not submitted a bid and as such that is true, but that is as much as I can say. I'm not prepared to breach any confidentiality.' Perhaps the most damning statement from Young was, 'It is true to say that the anonymous bidder will not want football to continue at Vale Park. In pure financial terms, the mystery bid is the highest offer so in those terms it would be the preferred bid.' The implication was that Stoke were to buy the club and wind it up, selling off the stadium and the land.

To briefly go back to one poignant quote from Arnold Bennett's *The Card*, 'The Directors had reluctantly come to the conclusion that they could not conscientiously embark on the dangerous risks of the approaching season, and that it was the intention of the Directors to wind up the club, in default of adequate public interest – when Bursley [Port Vale] read this in the Signal, the town was certainly shocked. Was the famous club, then, to disappear for ever, and the football ground to be sold in plots, and the grandstand for firewood?'

For many, the lack of a flat-out denial from the administrator was as good as a confirmation of the bid. The resounding response from all associated with Vale was of fear, anger and offence. Port Vale secretary Bill Lodey responded to the news through the official website with obvious disdain, 'The possibility of being merged with Stoke City to form one club would destroy the proud history of both clubs, and it would destroy what must be the most fierce rivalry between two sets of supporters, anywhere in the UK. The idea of moving from Vale Park to the Britannia Stadium must be something that could only be considered as a last resort.'

Paul McCann, a director of the fan-based Valiant 2001, contended, 'Stoke-on-Trent is parochial; we're fiercely attached to our towns – in Vale's case, Burslem. We might have accepted ground-sharing had the council built a stadium for both clubs, but not being dragged in by Stoke's owners to save money. We believe the club is sustainable, and want to hold it in trust, and make it healthy.'

Bill Bratt, who was leading the Valiant 2001 consortium, said, 'You only have to look at Stoke's monetary problems and how they treated the manager [Guðjón Thórdarson] who got them promoted. This must be stopped.'

Director Andrew Belfield declared, 'I am very shocked and totally opposed. The matter is in the hands of the Football League, but I would like fans to make as many protestations as possible to ensure football continues to be played at Vale Park.'

John Simmonds of the Sproson Trust supporters' group reacted to the rumours by saying, 'It's a calculated plan to create one club in the city and put Port Vale out of business,' while author and historical advisor Jeff Kent, at the time part of the Save the Vale fund, simply said, 'It's hard to believe anyone could come up with such a crass idea.'

The move by Young to make the bid public without officially making it public may have been an aggressive tactic to force one of the other genuine bidders to make their move and up their offer, essentially issuing an ultimatum: either buy the club, or lose it to your fiercest rivals. Bratt would lead the Valiant 2001 group to successfully take over the club in late 2002, quashing the Stoke merger rumours once and for all. The supporters' group beat off rival bids from Waterworld owner Mo Chaudry, Tunstall-based Summerbank Management, property development business partners Steve Ball and Iain McIntosh, what is assumed to be the anonymous bid from Stoke's Icelandic owners, and even a late bid from eccentric Italian businessman Gianni Paladini. Peter Walker of Valiant 2001 told BBC Radio Stoke, 'We're very pleased with the announcement and the hard work has paid off so far. We want it to be a club owned and run by its supporters.' Manager Brian Horton responded by admitting, 'It's been a worrying time. But the only thing we all want is to see football remain in Burslem.'

Other than securing the club's existence and taking Vale out of administration, other successes didn't really follow for Valiant 2001, on or off the pitch. The Valiants went close to making the Second Division play-offs in 2003/04, missing out on goal difference, but subsequent league performances generally went downhill as finances worsened once again. In 2007/08, under a trio of managers across the season (Martin Foyle, Dean Glover as caretaker and then Lee Sinnott), Vale finished second from bottom of the now-called League One, and were relegated to League Two.

* * *

After parting ways with the Valiants in 2002, Stoke would ride out the rest of the Icelandic years in typically bumpy fashion. Guðjón Thórdarson was sacked as manager just days after winning promotion, and his replacement, Steve Cotterill, walked out of the club weeks after walking in, as the owners were showing signs of looking for a way out. Tony Pulis was appointed thanks to the campaigning of the remaining English board members, keeping Stoke up when it seemed like an instant return to the Second Division was certain. After stabilising the Potters in mid-table in the First Division (which became the Championship for 2004/05 onwards), he was sacked in favour of one madcap season under Johan Boskamp.

The return of Peter Coates and Tony Pulis saw Stoke finally achieve promotion to the Premier League in 2008, where they would remain for the next ten years. As of 2008, Stoke and Vale were as far apart in league statuses as they could possibly be without one of the teams slipping out of the Football League altogether. Vale would win promotion in 2013, staying there for four seasons before relegation back to League Two in 2017. The following season, Stoke were relegated from the Premier League. At time of publication the clubs remain one division apart, with Vale having won promotion from League Two in 2021/22.

The good thing and bad thing about non-fictional books is that they capture a moment in time, and possibly everything leading up to that moment, but can only speculate on what may lie ahead. As beautiful as it can be to see how things once were, that also means they can be dated rather quickly. Speaking from my own professional experience as a geologist, there are textbooks and journals that were written before the global knowledge and acceptance of plate tectonics, something that is now taught to schoolkids as a generally accepted theory (if you aren't a flat-Earther anyway). In the context of this book, I sometimes wonder if it will get purchased in 2030, or even 2050, as a holographic projection in some charity shop in a levitating Longton precinct, now the de facto capital of the UK as the rest of the country is two feet below sea level. Actually, let's face it, Longton hasn't exactly changed much in the last 50 years; the only likely change in the next 50 is that Tesco expands to cover the entire town.

Anyway. I wonder what the state of play will be for the two Potteries teams, assuming both clubs live to see the next few decades and beyond. My thoughts wander to three possible situations: (1) Stoke City and

Port Vale still haven't met in league or cup; (2) Stoke and Vale have had a handful of encounters; (3) Stoke and Vale are regular league opponents. If (and let's face it, when) the two teams do meet again, I wonder how the rivalry will be received by fans both young and old, and how it will be perceived by the wider footballing community. As it stands here in the early 2020s, the sheer length of time apart and league differences really haven't done the Potteries derby rivalry any favours.

In fact, it begs an important question – is it even a rivalry anymore? Was it *ever* really a rivalry?

12

A Potteries Derby Retrospective

AS I'M writing this particular chapter in late 2021, I'm coming off a weekend of watching various football games, including the north London derby between Arsenal and Tottenham. Arsenal won 3-1, but I have to say, the whole thing was rather forgettable. Now I'm sure it probably doesn't feel that way for the matchday attendees in that part of the world, but as an outsider looking in, it just seemed like another in a long line of games between the two sides. They'll go on trading wins for countless seasons to come, just as they have for countless seasons that have passed, usually in a battle for who might finish sixth or seventh in the Premier League or something equally trivial.

I guess that's just football in some ways, especially in the modern era, where the richest of the rich compete with each other for a small selection of European places in 'the best league in the world'. I really don't mean to be dismissive of the north London derby, it's just the one that is freshest in my memory. Naturally it's because I'm writing this book, coupled with my obvious bias for my own club, that I feel like the Potteries derby has something special. But it's not just limited to our derby. When I think of the derbies I'd most like to watch as a neutral, I think of Birmingham City v Aston Villa in the Second City, or the Steel City derby in Sheffield between Wednesday and United. Maybe throw in the Black Country derby as Wolverhampton Wanderers face West Bromwich Albion, or even Newcastle v Sunderland, or Portsmouth v Southampton, despite these not being from the same cities. Is that just because of a general malaise that I have developed with the very 'top' clubs in England? Maybe; or perhaps it's because, for most of these derby clashes, there's usually a little bit more to it than just another league game for the same old league positions. For something like the Potteries derby, there are usually more narratives surrounding the game, more storytelling. Less like a European Super League, more an episode of WWE wrestling.

Sure, there are league positions on the line, and usually they matter. But they are not always contested under the same circumstances, in the same league, and for the same two or three positions, like say in a Manchester or Glasgow derby. We've had clashes across leagues that have involved both teams chasing promotion, both trying to avoid relegation, one of the two trying to go up or stay up, one trying to progress to the next round of the FA Cup, or even making the EFL Trophy matter. Then there are the little battles within the battle that develop, whether it be between larger-than-life players such as Mark Stein, Mike Sheron, Ian Bogie, Martin Foyle or Tony Naylor, or two iconic managers, in particular Lou Macari and John Rudge. The latter of course would also come to write his own interesting tale, switching to the red and white side of the city after 19 years in the black and white.

The arrival of the Icelanders added something new, something noteworthy. It gave an international element to the games, which again changed the narrative. I don't even need to go into the fan rivalries, the chants and waging battles across streets and pubs of the six towns. So, I think my position is quite clear. So why did I pose the earlier questions – is it a rivalry anymore, and was it ever really a rivalry?

Well, while I see that Stoke City and Port Vale not playing each other regularly is actually a reason to support our true rivalry status, others will disagree. If you're not playing each other, you're not really hating each other, right? Generationally, there are fans of both clubs that have never seen a real Potteries derby. In that time between 2002 and today, both clubs have developed new rivalries along the way, or rekindled old ones. For a while, Stoke fans would point to Cardiff City as a massive rival of ours, mainly during the Sam Hammam years where the two clubs fought for promotion, key players moved from Staffordshire to South Wales, and fans clashed violently. Once both teams had ultimately achieved their goals of promotion, the rivalry lessened with every encounter, until it became just another game.

The same happened with Burnley for a short period. Steve Cotterill, who controversially walked out of Stoke, saddled up at Burnley, who had also acquired several ex-Potters. There was never any 'true' rivalry, but there were some feisty encounters. Once again though, it passed. Then came the Premier League years, and the development of perhaps one rivalry that did persist – Arsenal. A cocktail of the Aaron Ramsey injury in 2010 and the subsequent fallout from Arsène Wenger, the reactions by both the injured Ramsey, the instigator Ryan Shawcross, Tony Pulis, Wenger, and of course, the fans of both clubs, mixed in with a string of bruising Stoke wins at the Britannia Stadium, meant that there was legitimate heat between the two clubs. Stoke's relegation has somewhat diluted that resentment, but it's still there. Along similar lines that fans would point to are other Midlands rivals – the likes of Wolves, West Brom and Derby County.

Vale have developed some strong rivalries with the more local teams that they would meet regularly in league fixtures, most notably of course Crewe Alexandra. The Alex have always been 'the other' local team, receiving coverage on BBC Radio Stoke and *The Sentinel*, so their presence is never too far from people's minds, no matter how one feels about them. Some fans embrace the north Staffordshire–south Cheshire rivalry, with some 13 miles separating the two teams, while others are quick to dismiss it as just another game, with the usual 'they care more about us than we do them' kind of retorts. Even David Artell, Crewe's manager from January 2017 to April 2022, waded in on the debate, saying, 'Who else have Vale got? Stoke? They haven't been in the same league as them for a very long time. I'm pretty sure they'd rather play us in a derby [than not have one].' Kind of sounds like a marriage of convenience rather than a true blood-thirsty rivalry.

In a 2019 study, 88 per cent of Crewe fans surveyed named Vale as their main rivals, followed by Stoke with 75 per cent. Stoke were considered Vale's number one rivals, named by 92 per cent of those surveyed, Crewe were second on 75 per cent. Incidentally, Vale were named Stoke's number one rival, but with 52 per cent, followed by Wolves, West Brom, Arsenal and Derby. Stoke were Arsenal's fourth-biggest rival, after Tottenham, Manchester United and Chelsea, as well as West Brom's fifth-biggest and Derby's-fourth biggest rival. That's a bit of a number soup, and these studies need to be taken with a pinch of salt, but to me, it suggests that the only true mutual rivals out of all of these teams chosen by Stoke and Vale fans were – Stoke and Vale. The others may bear resentment, but that may be stronger coming from one side than the other. Other teams that Vale can possibly identify as rivals in some capacity would be Walsall, Shrewsbury Town and Burton Albion, but I'd wager that these games generally lack the history and intensity of a true Potteries derby clash.

There are other indications that the Potteries derby is losing some of its ferocity, though. By 2017, local authorities were content with letting both teams play at home on the same afternoon, something that had typically been prevented since 1984, and even that was at different kick-off times. The two teams hadn't played at home at the same time since 1982. It's not a huge deal in the grand scheme of things; there is a thought that some matchday operators work both Stoke and Vale home games, which may have prevented this from happening before, but ultimately it's a police decision, and the police no longer saw any risk with both sets of fans making their way to games, congregating in towns and pubs, and making use of the local public transport.

Another way to see how the rivalry has changed is to take in what is being said on social media or, pray tell, the online forums. A brief look at the Stoke City online fan forum The Oatcake (not always a good idea, especially after a loss on matchday) still has a smattering of older threads about Port Vale from the early 2010s, and many fans are quick to claim that it's either a one-way rivalry (purely coming from the Vale side), or there is no rivalry at all. Then come the comparisons to the likes of West Brom, Wolves, and even Manchester United as our main rival. I actually saw someone on a Twitter poll suggest that *Sunderland* are bigger rivals to Stoke than Port Vale. Sunderland?! We know that many of these clubs wouldn't consider us in their top five rivalries, or in the case of Manchester United, care about us even less than that.

These kinds of responses remind me of a scene from the US TV drama series *Mad Men*. In one act, the main character Don Draper is in an elevator with a younger associate, Michael Ginsberg, who doesn't like Don or the way that he does business. After nearly a minute of lamenting Draper, Ginsberg ends his confrontation with, 'I feel bad for you.' Draper, masterfully portrayed by Jon Hamm, very nonchalantly responds with, 'I don't think about you at all,' and casually leaves the elevator. Kind of feels like Stoke fans are the Ginsberg in this analogy, and clubs like Manchester United and Wolves are Draper. Do we really want to be the kind of fans who are trying to pick fights with clubs that simply don't care about us? Especially in this cynical social media world of 'OBSESSED, RENT FREE, CRY MORE, RATIO' Twitter retorts.

With that in mind, that is how some Stoke fans see Vale supporters, as a pesky little Michael Ginsberg club who are trying to be our rivals. But do Vale fans even consider us rivals nowadays? Well, I can't speak for them, but I do speak *to* them from time to time. I wouldn't be writing this book if I didn't think the Potteries derby mattered and still matters to both sets of fans, and whenever I interact with my Port Vale friends and acquaintances, the 'hatred' for City still exists. There is no doubt that many still do care.

This was manifested after Stoke's relegation from the Premier League in 2018. As the story goes, a group of Port Vale fans had arranged for a plane to fly over both the bet365 Stadium (renamed for sponsorship reasons) and Vale Park, towing a banner saying 'WE STOOD THERE LAUGHING – PVFC'. Stoke's relegation was sealed at the bet365 on Saturday, 8 May 2018, going down 2-1 to Crystal Palace. However, there was no sign of the plane. In fact, the plane wouldn't fly over the respective grounds until the following weekend, with Vale's season already over and Stoke playing their final game the next day, 180 miles away at Swansea City. Of course, Stoke fans took to social media to mock the plane flying over two empty stadiums. The Vale response was to say that they couldn't be sure that Stoke's relegation would be confirmed on the previous weekend. The defence was also made that the plane still flew over the city, so the message was still sent. Perhaps the only defence worse than that was Stoke's back line in 2017/18. There was also the report that the plane flew a day early as Arsenal, of all teams, had booked it out for the day of the Swansea game in order to parade a couple of messages for outgoing manager Arsène Wenger and unpopular owner Stan Kroenke.

Alan Elliott, employed at the Blackpool-based firm air-ads.com, told *The Sentinel*, 'The person that booked us got in touch with us some weeks ago when it looked as though Stoke were going to go down. But obviously they wouldn't commit to this until they were sure. It was the Swansea game they wanted, but we had been booked for the banners being flown for Arsène Wenger over Huddersfield. So, the client asked if we would be prepared to fly it around Stoke on Saturday. We had a proposal banner on Southport beach at 1pm, so I said yes, we can but it would be late afternoon before we could get down and do it. They said yes fine, do that. We were over Stoke and the surrounding areas for around 45 minutes. I did both grounds, and it was a case of wander around the town centres which we did.'

The stunt reportedly cost £800 plus VAT. You could definitely argue that the banner received plenty of publicity, though it didn't exactly gain the kind that the group wanted. Still, they went to the effort to do it in the first place, and it wasn't exactly cheap. Wouldn't do that for a Walsall or a Burton. There was still time for one more deed; a couple of Valiants fans went down to the bet365 to tag it up with a sticker mocking the relegated team and manager Paul Lambert. Again though, it didn't really have the desired impact. The sticker was barely a couple of inches in length and width and was stuck on a lamp-post at the bottom end of the West Car Park, some 100 yards or so from the ground. The photo was again roundly mocked.

Of course, individual fan actions should not be generalised to represent the entire fanbase. Case in point: there was an incident during a Crewe v Vale game in November 2019 where a fan in a mid-1990s Stoke shirt ran on the pitch to taunt the travelling Valiants. The shirt included a number nine on the back, representing Paul Peschisolido, but rather than fork out a quid a letter on a name like that, the individual had chosen to simply go with 'PESCH'. Prudent!

There was the more noteworthy event that would display the level of rivalry that still exists. The preface that started this book – the EFL Trophy clash between Port Vale and Stoke's under-21s. Potters fans quickly snapped up the almost 4,000 tickets allocated to them, and they would have sold more if given the option. Some 180 officers were deployed for the clash in what Staffordshire Police described as their biggest footballing operation for ten years. The crowd of 7,940 was the highest at home that season for Port Vale. We all now know what transpired on the pitch, in the stands, in the concourse and in the streets that night.

Other than that, there was also a controversial commercial campaign launched by Vale in October 2019, where schoolchildren were offered the chance to swap their Stoke shirts and tickets for Vale ones, a response to Stoke's 'City 7s' scheme which gave seven-year-olds a replica shirt and match tickets for a game at the bet365 Stadium.

* * *

I sit here now, writing a day after Port Vale secured their place in the League Two play-off final (some time has passed since I started this chapter). A dramatic penalty shoot-out win against Swindon Town saw the jubilant Vale fans pour on to the pitch to celebrate the prospect of their first trip to the new Wembley, and potentially promotion back to League One. I have spent some time researching (reading Twitter) the reactions of Stoke fans to the result. There seems to be five types of Potters supporter: (1) those who do see Port Vale as a rival, and treat them as such (aka, not wanting to see them succeed); (2) those who do seem to have a genuine affection for the Valiants (well-wishers, 'good for the city' reasoning); (3) those who seem to be pretending to be happy for the Vale to save face ('good for the city' political line); (4) those who pretend to not care ('I didn't even look for the result', but secretly watched the entire 120-plus minutes); (5) those who genuinely don't care (watched Everton v Crystal Palace instead).

Stoke supporters – which one are you? I'd hazard a guess that the majority of those of a certain age, let's call them the late 'Generation Xers' and 'Millennials', either see Port Vale as rivals, or pretend not to care. These are the people who experienced the derbies of the 1990s and early 2000s, possibly the height of the rivalry in terms of hatred and competitiveness. For the early Gen X, 'Baby Boomer' and any pre-Second World War generations, I would guess that a high proportion are genuinely happy for Vale, having come up through the years of mixed fanbases, weekly ground hopping between the two clubs, friendly matches and helping each other out.

For the post-Millennial youngsters, there is probably a high element of passive interest, having never experienced a derby or any legitimate competition. For these fans, the minor interactions that the two teams have shared in the EFL Trophy and through the various superficial gestures are the only ways that the rivalry shows any signs of life. Ben Rowley of podcast *The YYY Files* is one such Stoke supporter who has never personally experienced a Potteries derby, so his own impressions of the rivalry have been forged from incidents in recent years. In Ben's own words, 'Having become a Stoke fan in 2009, my personal thoughts on Port Vale are both vague and convoluted. The two sides haven't played each other in the time I've followed football, aside from the meeting in the 2018/19 EFL Trophy. The carnage caused that day was infamous and, although I didn't attend, I was ashamed of the behaviour on display. The meeting itself was relatively insignificant, which implies those scenes would only be amplified in any proper future meeting between these sides. The rivalry between the two clubs is clearly fierce, albeit dormant, and this confuses me slightly.

'Stoke-on-Trent is a city personified by togetherness and graft despite circumstances; you could suggest that it wouldn't be amiss for the clubs to tentatively support each other (of which I seem to remember they have in certain recent off-the-field matters). And yet, not only is there no love lost between them, Stoke and Vale are each other's arch nemesis, and the feud is one of the most notorious in English football. There is probably recency bias for each to have new rivals (e.g., Arsenal for Stoke) but the potential for civil war between Stoke and Vale could not be overestimated if the two sides came within proximity of each other again. I'd love to know how the rivalry started, how it grew to such lengths along the way, and why the discontent persists despite the contest's slumber.'

As Ben alludes to, these very minor acts in recent years such as the EFL Trophy clash show that the rivalry is still there, simmering under the surface. Vale fan Patrick Floyd commented on that night, 'When Stoke fans sold out the away end, Norman Smurthwaite [Vale's chairman at the time] said he was going to give them the Paddock, and that got the Vale investment in, and it became fierce again. You saw early on in that game that the Stoke players weren't ready for it. Young lads at 17 or 18 getting grief when they went to take a throw-in. Tom Pope was obviously up for it! It was a great atmosphere. The Potteries derby is massively underrated; 2002 was the last time we played. You hear all about other derbies, there's probably about 38 derbies in London alone! There can't be many more cities where this many rival fans work together in a working-class area. The longer it goes on without a proper derby, not including 2018, the bigger it'll be.'

In many ways, thanks to the exploits of that night in 2018, the very thought of another Potteries derby leaves some fans feeling cold about the idea. *The Sentinel*'s Pete Smith gave his own thoughts on the current state of play and that EFL Trophy meeting, 'The gap between the rich and the poor or the quite rich and quite poor has grown and changed football so much since then and there's probably a generation of Stoke fans for whom Vale barely figure in their consciousness. Ryan Shawcross says he would have loved to have drawn Vale in a cup to get a taste of it but I'm not sure there would have been much to gain from a Stoke perspective if it had happened while they were in the Premier League. They either win and it's expected or it's a disaster.

'The tickets sold for the Football League Trophy game showed there was still an appetite for it all, but the aggression felt a bit manufactured. There was thuggish behaviour and vandalism rather than passion.'

Port Vale fan Barry Seaton summed it up by saying, 'As I write in October 2021, the next Potteries derby (league) is at least three years away. The three cup competitions afford chances of course, but many hope that the clubs avoid each other. The current young fanbase appears to be bitter, disenfranchised and violent. Carol Shanahan and Peter Coates deserve better.'

From the Potters' perspective, Angela Smith summed up her current feelings on the derby, 'I look back on those games and can still see the puddle of water that stopped Regis's goalbound effort, still feel the tension in the crowd at every game, the elation of winning, the despair of losing. Do I miss them? Yes. Do I want them to return? Not a chance. I prefer watching without that additional pressure these days.'

That feeling of enjoyable absence seems to be mutual across the divide, as Tom from the *Ale and the Vale* podcast notes, 'I fear the next derby will be horrific and full of trouble, as a lot of 27-year-olds and under haven't seen a derby.'

The age difference for some supporters may indeed be indicative of the dissimilarities in feeling and resentment levels between fans, as fellow podcast host Kirsty comments, 'The rivalry is different now. I have a laugh with Stoke fans and love reminding them about the 1990s when we were better. I don't hate Stoke like I used to, at all. There's a much bigger gulf between the two clubs and I like the fun banter now. It was different in the '90s. It might have been my age, but I honestly hated Stoke! And I loved it when we beat them!'

All that being said, there are many fans of different ages who would still love a chance to see the clubs go up against each other on a more even playing field (metaphorically, and also perhaps literally). Let's not pretend that Vale fans don't still revel in their 'you'll never beat the Vale' status, or that Stoke fans wouldn't love to get one over the Valiants in some kind of real cup tie. The EFL Trophy game may have even just made the prospect all that more enticing and intriguing, as Vale supporters' representative Ally Simcock reflected, 'I'm not sure there will ever be another Potteries derby like there used to be. However, you won't ever dampen the rivalry, it's ingrained in the city. You only have to look at the last cup game at Vale to see that.'

Ale and the Vale podcast co-host Dan would also welcome a renewal of the rivalry, but preferably on an even keel rather than in a cup tie: 'Now I still class Stoke as our closest rivals. However, it has been over 20 years since we last played them, and it's hard for a Vale fan to say, but we're a long way off being able to compete with them with the differences in money and revenue between the Championship and the leagues below. I'd love a Potteries derby again, but only when the clubs are on the same level. If we drew them in a cup game now, they would be big favourites.'

The prospect of meeting in the league right now isn't imminent, although it's more realistic than it was five years ago. Stoke have ebbed and flowed under Michael O'Neill and now Alex Neil in the Championship, and Vale are improving under Darrell Clarke and Andy Crosby, gaining promotion up to League One, just one league below the Potters at the time of writing. A league meeting between the two sides could be massive, especially if it is in the Championship. The last such fixture between the teams attracted 23,019, the highest attendance for a Potteries derby since 1992. It included a near-full away end, which, considering the South Stand at Stoke holds around 4,800, and Vale's average home attendance between 2002 and 2020 was typically between around 4,500 and 6,000, that's no mean feat. The appetite was there back in 2002, it was there in 2018 for a nothing EFL trophy match, it will be there whenever and wherever the two sides meet again. Perhaps next time, thanks to the history, the anticipation and the recent mini episodes between the two sets of supporters, the Potteries derby will get the national attention it deserves. Perchance next time there is a ranking, it'll come higher than Accrington Stanley v Morecambe.

When the next FA Cup draw that involves both teams comes around, I for one will be hoping for Stoke City v Port Vale. Then maybe we'll finally beat the Vale. Maybe.

Quotes about the Potteries derby

'Our fans only care about how hard they perform in the Port Vale shirt, how hard they work and are part of what we are building here. If they don't, whether they come from Stoke or Mars, it doesn't really matter. They need to make sure they are at it and giving all for the shirt because that is what our fans demand. Rivalry is good as well; they are our rivals. They are obviously streets ahead of us at the minute but, for me, if I think it is the right player, the right fit, the right time, Stoke are happy and we are happy, then we are happy.'

Darrell Clarke, Port Vale manager 2021–time of writing

'As much as some people would like to hype things up, if you're from Stoke-on-Trent you know there's only ever been one football derby worth talking about in these parts – and it doesn't involve Crewe Alexandra, Shrewsbury Town or another Midlands club.'

Martin Tideswell, ex-editor-in-chief of *The Sentinel*;
Port Vale Group communications director

'The Potteries derbies were phenomenal. I remember walking over Campbell Road and the atmosphere was electric. We could feel it. I'd had derbies before for Luton against Watford, but Stoke–Vale was something different.'

Mark Stein, Stoke City player 1991–93 and 1996–97

'One of the journalists from Radio Stoke was called George Andrews. One game against Port Vale, a derby match, I said to Neil [Baldwin], "If that b*stard comes down, don't let him in because he slagged the team off." I was joking. I'm sitting in the dugout at 3pm and security comes down and says, "George Andrews has been locked up in the laundry for two hours, should we let him out?"

'The game has kicked off and he's meant to be doing commentary for Radio Stoke. We go to the laundry and Nello has got him bound and gagged, tied to the chair.'

Lou Macari, Stoke City manager 1991–93 and 1994–1997

'I was very naive when I first came here because I didn't realise the clubs were so close in terms of location. When we played the first derby I was gobsmacked, 27,000 people there and you suddenly think, "Wooh!" It didn't take you long to realise how much it meant to everyone and it snowballed because we played them so many times in such a short period.'

Ian Cranson, Stoke City player 1989–96

'I did enjoy my celebration, and again I think that was because the crowd and the atmosphere at least made this feel like a proper derby. Had there just been a couple of hundred Stoke fans behind the goal then I would probably just have walked back to the halfway line, but the fact there were nearly 4,000 there – and they had been giving me plenty of stick – made it a bit different.'

Tom Pope, Port Vale player 2011–15 and 2017–21

'I think I'm still the last player to score for Stoke against the Vale, that's scary, but shows you how different the league positions have been.

'I never really knew how big the rivalry was until after I scored that goal. I never ripped up trees for Stoke but the fans have always been very appreciative and held me in high regard, as I do for them, because of goals like that. The Port Vale goal, when you look at what it meant and who it was against, is up there as my best goal.'

Chris Iwelumo, Stoke City player 2000–04

'Forget about nice lunches and nice pitches in the academy, you are up against lads who will rip your throat out to get to the ball.'

Robbie Earle, Port Vale player 1982–91

'Let's be honest, the atmosphere was fantastic. For those of us able to disseminate between banter and songs sung inside the ground, and the feeling to stupidly misbehave, this was a remarkable occasion and a vivid spectacle.'

Martin Smith, former *Oatcake* fanzine editor

'It was just a brilliant, brilliant, brilliant game, brilliant atmosphere, everything's electric. You feel the energy from the crowd, really urging you to win. Brilliant.'

Michael Cummins, Port Vale player 2000–06

'Port Vale had a very good team then and they were great occasions. It was always a privilege to play in them. It was always a good atmosphere at both grounds – whenever we went to Vale Park our travelling support was magnificent.'

Kevin Russell, Stoke City player 1992–93

'I would just say I have been very fortunate and very proud to have served both clubs. I've been lucky to have enjoyed some really exciting times with both.'

John Rudge, Port Vale manager 1983–99; club president 2019–time of writing; Stoke City director of football 1999–2013

'I didn't realise how great the rivalry was until we played each other for the first time. It is a massive game if the two teams ever play.'

Neil Aspin, Port Vale player 1989–99; manager 2017–19

'Staffordshire Police deployed over 200 officers after the Potters sold their entire 4,000 allocation in just two days.

'And they struggled to control the two sets of supporters who were baying for blood throughout the game.'

Dave Fraser, reporter for the *Scottish Sun*

'Port Vale, Stoke's big rivals but who they dwarfed in size, stayed up by a single point. I'm sure it must have been one of the darkest days in the club's history.'

Neville Southall, Stoke City player 1998

'Our fans would sooner see me shut the gates permanently than go in with Stoke.'

Bill Bell, Port Vale chairman 1987–2002

'If the Potteries derby had never happened, we would have £80,000 to put back into policing.'

Matthew Ellis, Staffordshire's commissioner for police, fire and rescue, and crime

'At Port Vale, we try very hard to limit the number of police inside the ground and try to manage ourselves, but obviously the game against Stoke is a very different kettle of fish.'

Ally Simcock, Port Vale fans' liaison officer; former chairwoman of the Port Vale Supporters' Club

'I never really understood the bitterness that existed between the two clubs among supporters. I suppose I could be accused of condescension here, but Vale, especially at that time [the 1970s], were a lower-league club. At a time when Stoke, under the management of Tony Waddington, were performing at the highest level. I will say that I admire supporters who support their local clubs in their hometowns. If I had been born in Packmoor or Stanfield I would, probably, be a Vale fan.'

Bill Cawley, historian and Stoke City fan

'A study has caught our eye ranking the top 30 derbies in the top four divisions of English football. It puts Stoke City and Port Vale at joint 28th, level with

Manchester United v Manchester City. The same study puts Portsmouth–Southampton at number one, keeping Exeter City–Plymouth Argyle and Arsenal–Tottenham Hotspur off the top spot. Port Vale v Crewe Alexandra comes in at 14th. Now we are certain that you'll disagree.'

Pete Smith, Stoke City reporter for *The Sentinel*

'When will they meet again? Vale fans would wish it to be next season as it would mean promotion, whereas Stoke fans would understandably be horrified at the suggestion considering their present league position. Who knows when it will be, but you never know, it is bound to happen one day!'

Phil Sherwin, author and historian

'The Potteries derby is a bigger historic rivalry than Protestants v Catholics.'

Pope Francis, probably

Acknowledgments

ONCE AGAIN, I am extremely grateful to Jane Camillin, and all at Pitch Publishing, for giving me the opportunity to publish this book on yet another niche local football topic, albeit further extended to the greater Potteries footballing universe. I'm also ever-appreciative of my dad Dave and brother David, the fountains of Stoke City knowledge, for their help and support.

I wish to thank all the contributors and those that have offered their time and expertise on the Potteries Derby, including Ally Simcock, Patrick Floyd, Barry Seaton, Tom Amos, Dan Berrisford, Kirsty Rollings, Angela Smith, Pete Smith, Ben Rowley and Carl Dickinson. I'm particularly indebted to Patrick, Angela and Pete for opening doors on both the north and south sides of the city, and to Carl for writing the foreword. As always, The Sentinel has been the go-to source for all things Stoke City and Port Vale over the years, as well as articles in Duck Magazine, The Oatcake, onevalefan.co.uk, KnotFM and BBC Radio Stoke. Thanks as well to Tom Cooper for his unwavering support (good luck with the Wolves book!) and my friends out here in Gran Alacant, Mike and Gerry, for their constant words of encouragement on late *late* nights in Jolly's and Miley's ("he wrote a boo-oo-ook you know!"). ¡*Mucho Elche!*

Last but not least, thank you to my beautiful wife Cris – always my team-mate and never my rival.

Afterword

By the way, I guess the title should actually be *La Cerámica* if we're using real Spanish, but then it wouldn't be a play on *El Clásico*, would it? I would like to take credit for the title, but I'm sure I heard it via the *Wizards of Drivel* podcast, who in turn may have heard it via someone else. In 2016, Sam Wallace of *The Telegraph* referred to a hypothetical game between Villarreal (who play their home games at Estadio de la Cerámica, or in English, the Ceramics Stadium) and Stoke. Several other social media users have claimed to have come up with it too! Anyway, I will give credit to the Wizards for putting this into the Potteries zeitgeist. Much like *Twinned with Reykjavik*, I get my book titles from much more creative supporters than myself.

Bibliography

The Sentinel/Stoke-on-Trent Live Articles

16 Nov 2017: Michael Baggaley - Port Vale and Stoke City to stage home games on same day https://www.stokesentinel.co.uk/sport/football/port-vale-stoke-city-stage-784841

24 Nov 2017: Michael Baggaley - 25 years on from Port Vale 3, Stoke City 1, and two Potteries teams to be proud of https://www.stokesentinel.co.uk/sport/football/25-years-port-vale-3-824736 .

24 Nov 2017: Michael Baggaley - 'My biggest regret is I couldn't return the favour!' Port Vale's Neil Aspin on THAT challenge by Stoke City's Steve Foley https://www.stokesentinel.co.uk/sport/football/my-biggest-regret-couldnt-return-825146

3 Dec 2017: Peter Smith - Did you notice? Rare photo as Stoke City and Port Vale stage home games on same day for first time since 1984 https://www.stokesentinel.co.uk/sport/football/football-news/stoke-city-port-vale-photo-869519

14 Jan 2018: Michael Baggaley - When Port Vale gave Arsenal an almighty FA Cup scare https://www.stokesentinel.co.uk/sport/football/port-vale-arsenal-fa-cup-1063053

3 Mar 2018: Michael Baggaley - Happy anniversary Port Vale 25 years on from Autoglass Trophy win at Stoke City https://www.stokesentinel.co.uk/sport/football/happy-anniversary-port-vale-25-1280949

12 May 2018: Keith Wales - Port Vale plane finally takes to the air to mock Stoke City's relegation from the Premier League https://www.stokesentinel.co.uk/sport/football/football-news/stoke-city-port-vale-plane-1560986

22 May 2018: Michael Baggaley - Are you on our pictures? Port Vale win the Autoglass Trophy at Wembley 25 years ago today https://www.stokesentinel.co.uk/sport/football/football-news/gallery/you-pictures-port-vale-win-1583719

4 Dec 2018: Peter Smith - Stoke City fans condemn behaviour 'that should have been left in 1980s' after chaos at Port Vale https://www.stokesentinel.co.uk/sport/football/football-news/port-vale-stoke-city-checkatrade-2292625

5 Dec 2018: Peter Smith - 55 photos from dramatic night on and off pitch as Port Vale beat Stoke City u21s https://www.stokesentinel.co.uk/sport/football/football-news/gallery/55-photos-dramatic-night-pitch-2294322

7 Dec 2018: Richard Ault - Revealed: Policing the Potteries derby has cost YOU £80k https://www.stokesentinel.co.uk/news/stoke-on-trent-news/revealed-policing-potteries-derby-cost-2298995

18 Jan 2019: Michael Baggaley - Twenty years today - Port Vale part company with greatest manager John Rudge https://www.stokesentinel.co.uk/sport/football/football-news/twenty-years-today-port-vale-2436978

4 May 2019: Peter Smith - 10 things you probably didn't know about Stoke City's old Victoria Ground - 22 years since the final game https://www.stokesentinel.co.uk/sport/football/football-news/facts-stoke-city-victoria-ground-1997886

8 Aug 2019: David Dubas-Fisher - REVEALED: Port Vale v Stoke City u21s had highest known police presence for any game in country last season https://www.stokesentinel.co.uk/sport/football/football-news/port-vale-stoke-city-police-3195162

9 Sep 2019: Peter Smith - Stoke City v Port Vale named in top 30 rivalries in English football - below Vale v Crewe Alexandra https://www.stokesentinel.co.uk/sport/football/football-news/stoke-city-port-vale-derby-3300121

23 Sep 2019: Michael Baggaley - Thirty years today - Port Vale resume rivalries with Stoke City at packed Victoria Ground https://www.stokesentinel.co.uk/sport/football/football-news/port-vale-stoke-city-pictures-3350040

25 Sep 2019: Michael Baggaley - Robbie Earle - The Stoke City game when we were no longer 'little old Port Vale' https://www.stokesentinel.co.uk/sport/football/football-news/stoke-city-port-vale-earle-3360585

29 Jan 2020: Peter Smith - 'It was electric' - Mark Stein on Stoke City-Port Vale derbies, that penalty and the goal that send fans crazy https://www.stokesentinel.co.uk/sport/football/football-news/stoke-port-vale-mark-stein-1507088

6 Mar 2020: Michael Baggaley - Robbie Earle - 'I'll happily wait longer for the next Port Vale v Stoke City game' https://www.stokesentinel.co.uk/sport/football/football-news/robbie-earle-port-vale-stoke-3924854

6 Mar 2020: Michael Baggaley - 'When will Stoke City and Port Vale meet again?' - 100 years since first league derby https://www.stokesentinel.co.uk/sport/football/football-news/stoke-city-port-vale-derby-3920555

6 Mar 2020: Peter Smith - 'Let's see how your bottle is' - Top three Stoke City wins over Port Vale https://www.stokesentinel.co.uk/sport/football/football-news/stoke-city-port-vale-stein-3920601

23 Apr 2020: Peter Smith - Neville Southall on Stoke City, Chris Kamara and 'one of the worst episodes of my life' https://www.stokesentinel.co.uk/sport/football/football-news/stoke-city-neville-southall-kamara-4073637

29 Apr 2020: Peter Smith - Stoke City 1 Plymouth Argyle 0 as it happened! Pitch invasion as Peter Fox double save, Nigel Gleghorn goal seal title https://www.stokesentinel.co.uk/sport/football/match-reports/stoke-city-plymouth-pitch-invasion-4085688

3 May 2020: Michael Baggaley - Last day drama when Port Vale stayed up but Man City and Stoke City went down https://www.stokesentinel.co.uk/sport/football/football-news/last-day-drama-port-vale-4100853

24 Oct 2020: Peter Smith - Stoke City 2 Port Vale 1 in 65 pictures - Mark Stein penalty, pitch invaders and blood and thunder action https://www.stokesentinel.co.uk/sport/football/football-news/gallery/stoke-city-2-port-vale-2142040

2 Nov 2020: Peter Smith - The inside story of Stoke City, Coventry and note that sparked John Rudge and Johan Boskamp rift https://www.stokesentinel.co.uk/sport/football/football-news/stoke-john-rudge-johan-boskamp-717927

3 Nov 2020: Peter Smith - Stoke City record breaker Mike Sheron explains why Norwich boss Martin O'Neill swapped him for Keith Scott https://www.stokesentinel.co.uk/sport/football/transfer-news/stoke-city-transfer-mike-sheron-4663614

14 Nov 2020: Tom Pope - 'You can imagine how my group chat with Stoke fans went' - Port Vale's Tom Pope https://www.stokesentinel.co.uk/sport/football/football-news/you-can-imagine-how-group-4698947

4 Jan 2022: Peter Smith - Was this the worst night in Stoke City's history? https://www.stokesentinel.co.uk/sport/football/football-news/stoke-city-butler-street-roof-1008179

31 Mar 2022: Peter Smith - Port Vale 0 Stoke City 2 - Grobbelaar, Stein and packed away end in 33 pictures from 1993 classic derby https://www.stokesentinel.co.uk/sport/football/football-news/gallery/port-vale-0-stoke-city-1406510

3 May 2022: Peter Smith - Mayhem and 'fighting everywhere' as Stoke and Man City are relegated - 24 years on https://www.stokesentinel.co.uk/sport/football/football-news/stoke-manchester-city-relegated-1998-2832019

Independent Articles

31 Mar 1993: Phil Shaw - Football: Record run ends in Vale of tears https://www.independent.co.uk/sport/football-record-run-ends-in-vale-of-tears-1452721.html

16 May 1993: Phil Andrews - Football: Glover pushes Vale back into the frame: Barclays League promotion play-offs, semi-finals https://www.independent.co.uk/sport/football-glover-pushes-vale-back-into-the-frame-barclays-league-promotion-playoffs-semifinals-2323396.html

19 May 1993: Jon Culley - Football League Play-Offs: Vale manage to find perfect Foyle https://www.independent.co.uk/sport/football-league-playoffs-vale-manage-to-find-perfect-foyle-2324109.html

31 May 1993: Phil Shaw - Football / Play-Off: Albion exploit Vale's misfortune: Swan's dismissal opens the door to the First Division for Ardiles' men https://www.independent.co.uk/sport/football-play-albion-exploit-vale-s-misfortune-swan-s-dismissal-opens-door-first-division-ardiles-men-2316240.html

27 Aug 1995: Phil Shaw - Valiant Bogie proves a bargain https://www.independent.co.uk/sport/valiant-bogie-proves-a-bargain-1598431.html

20 Apr 1997: Phil Shaw - Football: Sheron casts veil over Rudge's hopes https://www.independent.co.uk/sport/football-sheron-casts-veil-over-rudge-s-hopes-1268386.html

12 Oct 1997: Football: Stoke profit from Keen's capability https://www.independent.co.uk/sport/football-stoke-profit-from-keen-s-capability-1235614.html

8 Apr 1998: Andrew Martin -Football: Kamara leaves struggling Stoke https://www.independent.co.uk/sport/football-kamara-leaves-struggling-stoke-1155373.html

18 Sep 2000: Phil Shaw - Lightbourne to Stoke's rescue https://www.independent.co.uk/sport/football/football-league/lightbourne-to-stoke-s-rescue-700926.html

1 Feb 2003: Phil Shaw - Stoke owners in bid for Port Vale https://www.independent.co.uk/sport/football/football-league/stoke-owners-in-bid-for-port-vale-117569.html

8 Feb 2003: David Conn - Icelanders draw veil over Stoke groundshare https://www.independent.co.uk/sport/football/news/david-conn-icelanders-draw-veil-over-stoke-groundshare-118345.html

BBC News Articles

12 Jan 1998: Hundreds protest after 7-0 drubbing http://news.bbc.co.uk/2/hi/sport/football/46421.stm

17 Sep 2000: Port Vale 1-1 Stoke City http://news.bbc.co.uk/sport2/hi/football/eng_div_2/929076.stm

223

26 Sep 2000: Vale will not merge http://news.bbc.co.uk/sport2/hi/football/eng_div_2/942844.stm

29 Dec 2000: Port Vale not facing 'cash crisis' http://news.bbc.co.uk/sport2/hi/football/teams/p/port_vale/1092736.stm

21 Oct 2001: Port Vale 1-1 Stoke City http://news.bbc.co.uk/sport2/hi/football/eng_div_2/1608735.stm

21 Oct 2002: Clubs in crisis https://www.bbc.co.uk/insideout/westmidlands/series1/football-finance.shtml

19 Dec 2002: Vale in Robbie plea http://news.bbc.co.uk/1/hi/england/2591737.stm

22 Jan 2003: Robbie says 'no' to Port Vale http://news.bbc.co.uk/1/hi/england/2682589.stm

31 Jan 2003: Vale deny Potters merger http://news.bbc.co.uk/sport2/hi/football/teams/p/port_vale/2713971.stm

5 Feb 2003: Vale Park fears rise http://news.bbc.co.uk/sport2/hi/football/teams/p/port_vale/2730111.stm

19 Feb 2003: Fans take over Port Vale http://news.bbc.co.uk/sport2/hi/football/teams/p/port_vale/2779709.stm

5 Apr 2006: John Rudge - the "quiet man" https://www.bbc.co.uk/stoke/content/articles/2006/04/05/local_heroes_john_rudge_feature.shtml

13 May 2009: Brammer denied new Vale contract http://news.bbc.co.uk/sport2/hi/football/teams/p/port_vale/8048691.stm

5 Dec 2018: Port Vale 4-0 Stoke City U21 https://www.bbc.co.uk/sport/football/46451780

onevalefan Articles

29 Jan 2012: Bogie: Thanks for the support https://web.archive.org/web/20160202162007/http:/www.onevalefan.co.uk/site/2012/01/bogie-support/

31 Jan 2012: The Potteries derbies https://www.onevalefan.co.uk/2012/01/potteries-derbies/

17 Nov 2014: Listen: Managing Vale by Sir Stanley Matthews https://www.onevalefan.co.uk/2014/11/listen-managing-vale-by-sir-stanley-matthews/

3 Dec 2016: Cult Hero 62: Arthur Bridgett https://www.onevalefan.co.uk/2016/12/cult-hero-62-arthur-bridgett/

10 Jan 2020: Why are they called Port Vale? https://www.onevalefan.co.uk/2020/01/why-called-port-vale/

YouTube Channels

onevalefan - independent Port Vale news and views https://www.youtube.com/user/onevalefan

PortValeOnline https://www.youtube.com/channel/UCF2o4HkdfD4-9Vdlv3tRJAA

Other Sources

18 Apr 2019: Colin Burgess (Stoke City FC Official) - We've Got History: Middlesbrough https://www.stokecityfc.com/news/weve-got-history-middlesbrough

16 Sep 2019: Martyn Cooke (Playing Pasts) - 'A chastening experience': When Sir Stanley Matthews managed Port Vale Football Club https://www.playingpasts.co.uk/articles/football/a-chastening-experience-when-sir-stanley-matthews-managed-port-vale-football-club/

18 Feb 2001: Mike Prestage (The Guardian) - Vale thwart rivals https://www.theguardian.com/football/Observer_Match_Report/0,,-33815,00.html

19 Feb 2001: Ian Bayley (The Guardian) - Potters armed but not dangerous https://www.theguardian.com/football/2001/feb/19/match.sport13

5 Mar 2001: Stuart James (Sky Sports) - Vale prevail in derby https://www.skysports.com/football/news/2205552/vale-prevail-in-derby

10 Aug 2001: Valiant 2001 critical of Brammer sale https://web.archive.org/web/20021012065737/http:/www.valiant2001.com/html/press/10082001.htm

14 May 2018: Michael Baggaley and Alex Smith (Mirror) - How Arséne Wenger stopped cheeky Port Vale fans' plane banner mocking rivals Stoke City over relegation https://www.mirror.co.uk/sport/football/news/how-arsene-wenger-stopped-cheeky-12534623

5 Dec 2018: Joe Moore (talkSPORT) - DERBY MAYHEM - Port Vale supporter chief SLAMS Stoke City fans after derby chaos: 'It was absolute carnage'https://talksport.com/football/efl/456366/port-vale-stoke-city-fans-derby-chaos/

Fan Banter - The top five rivals of English football's top 92 clubs revealed https://fanbanter.co.uk/the-top-five-rivals-of-english-footballs-top-92-clubs-revealed/

21 Sep 2018: Peter Morse (CheshireLive) - Crewe Alex versus Port Vale: Is it a derby? Here's what David Artell thinks https://www.cheshire-live.co.uk/sport/football/crewe-alex-versus-port-vale-15182846